A
COMMONPLACE BOOK
of
COOKERY

*To suckle fools and
chronicle small
beer.*

SHAKESPEARE

A
COMMONPLACE BOOK
of
COOKERY

A COLLECTION of Proverbs, Anecdotes, Opinions
and Obscure Facts on Food, Drink, Cooks,
Cooking, Dining, Diners & Dieters,
dating from ancient times
to the present,
compiled
by

ROBERT GRABHORN
and with a PREFACE by M. F. K. FISHER

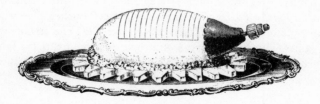

NORTH POINT PRESS : San Francisco : 1985

ACKNOWLEDGMENTS

Permission has been granted to use material from the following works. Every reasonable effort has been made to clear the use of the material in this volume with copyright owners.

Once around the Sun, Brooks Atkinson; *Any Number Can Play*, Clifton Fadiman (World Publishing); *The American Credo*, George Jean Nathan & H. L. Mencken, and *Prejudices*, H. L. Mencken (Copyright Alfred A. Knopf, Inc.); *Bertolt Brecht: Collected Plays* (Copyright Pantheon Books, a Division of Random House, Inc.); *The Essential Gandhi*, ed. by Louis Fischer (Copyright Random House, Inc.); *Verses from 1929 On*, Copyright 1930 by Ogden Nash; *The Almost Perfect State*, by Don Marquis, *Please Don't Eat the Daisies*, by Jean Kerr (Copyright Doubleday & Co., Inc.); *Man the Unknown*, by Alexis Carrel, *Inside Benchley*, by Robert Benchley, *Letters to his Nephew*, by Arnold Bennett (Harper & Row); *Anatomy of a Murder*, by Robert Traver (St. Martin's Press, Inc.); *Collected Poems*, by G. K. Chesterton, *Golden Fleece*, by William Rose Benet (Dodd, Mead & Co., Inc.); *Remember to Remember*, by Henry Miller, Copyright 1947 by New Directions Publishing Corp. Reprinted by permission of New Directions Publishing Corp.; *A Room of One's Own*, by Virginia Woolf, *The Road to Wigan Pier*, by George Orwell (Harcourt, Brace, Jovanovich); *Poems in Praise of Practically Nothing*, by Samuel Hoffenstein (Liveright Publishing Corp.); *Further Fables of Our Time*, by James Thurber, Copyright 1956 by James Thurber (Simon & Schuster); *The Thurber Carnival*, by James Thurber, (Harper & Row), Copyright 1945, James Thurber, Copyright 1973, Helen W. Thurber and Rosemary Thurber Sauers.

CONTENTS

PREFACE
by
M. F. K. FISHER

FOR anyone addicted to reading commonplace books, which are rarely compiled by commonplace people, of course, finding a good new one is much like enduring a familiar recurrence of malaria, with fever, fits of shaking, strange dreams. Unlike a truly paludismic ordeal, however, the symptoms felt while savoring a collection of one man's pet quotations are voluptuously enjoyable, as I have found lately with Robert Grabhorn's deep and tantalizing book.

The usual fever is one of enjoyment, in recognizing old favorites and familiar sentences I myself would certainly have included . . . if ever I had got to the brutal point of making my own collection with dedication rather than dawdling. And the shakings are based on both envy and shock, at what Grabhorn often chose, and why this or that utterly valueless triviality clutters his pages, and where he missed an extraordinary jewel such as I would have tucked in. And the strange dreams, feverish and shaky, are naturally about my own unwritten commonplace book, one such as never before has been put together, a distillation of humankind's purest spirit, an intuitive (and egomanic!) appreciation of all the wise wit of our centuries (and a lasting monument to my own!).

Countless readers have fallen victim to this form of

intellectual infection, fortunately for the rest of us who realize that we could or should have succumbed, no matter how modestly and privately, but who were well dosed instead with the quinine of ambition, or of social inertia. All we can be is grateful, as we feverishly, shakily (dreamily, jealously, scornfully, delightedly) read what others have compiled, from their own long readings.

Mr. Grabhorn, who was born in 1900 and died after a fine full life in 1973, did just such a job for the rest of us lazier lovers of what others have said better than we could. (Envious as we are of the fellow-sufferer who actually got his compilation onto paper, we at least chuckle and sigh and agree . . . most of the time.)

Robert Grabhorn began his clipping early, and during his lifetime collected at least eight volumes of quotations on printing alone, and the prospect of editing and/or reading them should raise the temperature of any press-paludist. He was about thirty, though, and well along in his rich life, before he began to pluck gastronomical crumbs from off and from under the tables of the great, sub-great, superficial wits and thinkers of History, and he did not stop this delicious habit until a few days before he died.

It probably began when his elder brother and printing partner Edwin sent him to Europe for a year, in 1923-24. Of course he studied bookbinding and observed presses and such-like there, but he also worked diligently at the arts of eating and drinking. Then,

back in America, he married the "brilliant and out-
rageous" Jane, with whom he zealously continued
his full curriculum. She undoubtedly whetted his
fever for collecting quotations that could stimulate
or amuse or even irritate him (which is what most
commonplace books are for, of course).

Plainly Robert Grabhorn used his clipping habit,
subconsciously or not, but on every subject that interested him, as an educational tool. He had never
graduated from college, but kept learning until he
died, fighting jauntily with his self-forged weapons.

He and Jane, who at one point founded her own
Jumbo Press to spoof all such fine printing as the
Grabhorns turned out with intuitive taste and skill,
made a firm custom of "going out" at least three
times every week, to restaurants and night-spots.
They were familiars of North Beach in San Francisco,
which was even more intensely riotous in their time
than it is now. They ate with insatiable enjoyment,
drank plentifully and well, and never, or almost never
let their roisterings interfere with the next morning's
session, press-side.

Once, though, they missed a day's work, according
to their friend Porter Garnett, the great printer-de-
signer. He was disturbed not to find them at the
offices, and went to their place on Russian Hill. There
they lay side by side in their big bed, rigid and speech-
less with rage at each other. They had been either
bowling or playing bocce-ball early in the morning
on upper Broadway, he learned in surly snarls. Bob

had dropped a ball on Jane's foot. Then she had in some way (Garnett was a very discreet friend, especially about ladies) injured her playmate in retaliation. And there they lay, implacably not speaking to each other, not touching . . . until it was time either to hobble out again for dinner or welcome the floating population of thirsty hungry voluble companions who filled their nights at home.

An incident like this may seem to have little to do with Mr. Grabhorn's steady and perhaps stubborn compilation of his private commonplace books, all the while his presses were printing more than 500 beautiful volumes. Myself, I do not think it is trivial. It is part of the reasons for his choices of quotations. While he lay silent, bruised, and enraged, he may well have been choosing several new titbits for his little book:

> *My soul is dark with stormy riot,*
> *Directly traceable to diet.*

Samuel Hoffenstein said that, and it rang with new truth. And Aléxandre Dumas once quipped profoundly about a bibulous absentee from a business conference,

> *. . . he absinthes himself a bit too much . . .*

and then H. L. Mencken observed all too cogently,

> *No man is genuinely happy, married, who has to drink worse gin than he used to drink when he was single.*

It seems quite probable to me that after a little more of this wry medicine, Mr. Grabhorn could give Jane a slap and a tickle, rise from his bed, and repair immediately to his desk-drawer where the Cookery collection hid . . . and that then he and his wife limped back to life, back to the presses . . .

Among the several reactions to a good commonplace book of anyone infected with the virus, few are truly negative, and the meanest of us is genuinely delighted when a special quotation has made the grade in another man's book (as I was when I saw an inimitable line from Daisy Ashford's *The Young Visitors* just where I would have put it in the Grabhorn . . .). But probably the best thing about such shared reading is the relationship with the one who made it possible, the one who did the clipping, the sorting. It is not presumptuous, but it is usually personal and even intimate.

I never met Robert Grabhorn or Jane or Brother Edwin, but I have long been aware and appreciative of what they did for printing and fine publishing in the modern world, and through mutual friends I have relished stories of their vigorous lives in and out of the press rooms. And now, cheated by both Time and Circumstance but rescued by Robert's consuming fever for the written word, I know him well! He garnered what I too would have, given his lusty curiosity and lack of sloth, about fingerbowls, sauerkraut, garbage, milk and Scotch and wine and beer and even Temperance, eggs, teeth, politics, cocktail olives, poverty, garlic, remorse and love . . . Plainly he was a man of more than our common spiritual grace and good humor, and a good one to know, then and now.

A
COMMONPLACE BOOK
of
COOKERY

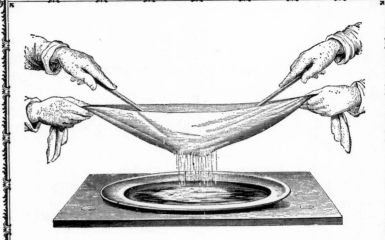

# of COOKS
AND COOKING

THE greatest animal in creation, the animal who cooks.   DOUGLAS JERROLD, 1803-1857

A cook they hadde with hem for the nones
To boille the chicknes with the marybones,
And poudre-marchant tart, and galingale.
Wel coude he know a draughte of London ale.
He coude roste, and sethe, and broille,
Maken mortreux, and wel bake a pye. . . .
For blankmanger, that made he with the beste.

GEOFFREY CHAUCER, 1340?-1400, *Canterbury Tales*

Oh, I am a cook and a captain bold,
  And the mate of the Nancy brig,
And a bo'sun tight, and a midshipmite,
  And the crew of the captain's gig.
w. s. GILBERT, 1836-1911, The Bab Ballads

We may live without poetry, music and art;
We may live without conscience, and live without
  heart;
We may live without friends, we may live without
  books;
But civilized man cannot live without cooks.
OWEN MEREDITH, 1831-1891, Lucile

Woman does not understand what food means, and
yet she insists upon being a cook!
F. W. NIETZSCHE, 1844-1900, Beyond Good and Evil

Women cannot make a good book of cookery.
SAMUEL JOHNSON, 1709-1784

Until the nature of man is completely altered, cooking is the most important thing for a woman.
ARNOLD BENNETT ,1867-1911

Kissing don't last: cookery do.
GEORGE MEREDITH, 1828-1909

Cooking is like love. It should be entered into with
abandon or not at all.   HARRIET VAN HORNE, 1920-

A woman who leaves her cook never wholly recovers her position in Society.   SAKI, 1870-1916

All the best cooks and dressmakers are men.
MENCKEN & NATHAN, *The American Credo*, 1920

Cookery is become an art, a noble science: cooks are gentlemen.
ROBERT BURTON, 1577-1540, *Anatomy of Melancholy*

When I make a feast,
I would my guests praise it, not the cooks.
SIR JOHN HARINGTON, 1561-1612

His cook is his chief merit. The world visits his dinners, not him.   MOLIERE, 1622-1673, *Le Misanthrope*

The French would be the best cooks in Europe if they had got any butcher's meat.
WALTER BAGEHOT, 1826-1877, *Biographical Studies*

Cooks are made, roasters are born.   FRENCH PROVERB

When a cook cooks a fly he keeps the best wing for himself.   POLISH PROVERB

I have always thought geniuses much inferior to the plain sense of the cookmaid, who can make a good pudding and keep the kitchen in order.
MARY WORTLEY MONTAGU, 1689-1762

Plain cooking cannot be trusted to plain cooks.

COUNTESS MORPHY

The cook was a good cook as cooks go; and as cooks go she went. SAKI, 1870-1916

A good cook is a certain slow poisoner, if you are not temperate. VOLTAIRE, 1694-1778, *Philosophical Dictionary*

Our God is great and the cook is his prophet.

JEROME K. JEROME, 1855-1927, *Idle Thoughts of an Idle Fellow*

God sends meat and the devil sends cooks.

ENGLISH PROVERB

I seem to you cruel and too much addicted to gluttony, when I beat my cook for sending up a bad dinner. If that seems to you too trifling a cause, pray tell for what cause you would have a cook flogged.

MARTIAL, *c*. A.D. 40-104, *Epigrammata*

It is no wonder that diseases are innumerable: count the cooks.

SENECA, 4 B.C.?-A.D. 65, *Epistulae morales ad Lucilium*

Too many cooks spoil the broth. ENGLISH PROVERB

Bad cooks—and the utter lack of reason in the kitchen—have delayed human development longest and delayed it most. FRIEDRICH NIETZSCHE, 1844-1900

Man is a cooking animal. The beasts have memory, judgement, and all the faculties and passions of our mind, in a certain degree; but no beast is a cook.

JAMES BOSWELL, 1740-1790, *Tour to the Hebrides*

There is a higher average of good cooking at Oxford and Cambridge than elsewhere. The dinners are better than the curriculum. But there is no chair of cookery; it is taught by apprenticeship in the kitchen.

SAMUEL BUTLER, 1835-1902

The taste of the kitchen is better than the smell.

THOMAS FULLER, 1608-1661, *Gnomology*

Cooking: Home-made dishes that drive one from the house.   THOMAS HOOD, 1798-1845

Cooking is half-digesting; we do half our digestion, therefore, outside our bodies.

SAMUEL BUTLER, 1835-1902

Frying gives cooks numerous ways of concealing what appeared the day before, and in a pinch facilitates sudden demands, for it takes little more time to fry a four-pound carp than to boil an egg.

BRILLAT-SAVARIN, 1755-1826, *Physiologie du Goût*

The receipts of cookery are swelled to a volume; but a good stomach excels them all.

WILLIAM PENN, 1644-1718, *Fruits of Solitude*

o_f EATING

I<small>F</small> you are ever at a loss to support a flagging conversation, introduce the subject of eating.

LEIGH HUNT, 1784-1859, Table Talk

Every man should eat and drink, and enjoy the good of all his labour; it is the gift of God.

Ecclesiastes iii, 13

Soup and fish explain half the emotions of life.

SYDNEY SMITH, 1771-1845

What is patriotism but the love of the good things we ate in our childhood.

LIN YUTANG, 1895-1976

The discovery of a new dish does more for human happiness than the discovery of a new star.

BRILLAT-SAVARIN, 1755-1826, *Physiologie du Goût*

Some like it hot,
Some like it cold,
Some like it in the pot,
Nine days old.   NURSERY RHYME, *c.* 1850

To eat well is no Whoredom; and to starve is no Gentility.   THOMAS FULLER, 1608-1661, *Gnomology*

"Do you know when there will be a world famine?" "When the Chinese learn to eat with forks and spoons."   TOPICAL RUSSIAN JOKE

Good to eat, and wholesome to digest, as a worm to a toad, a toad to a snake, and a snake to a pig, a pig to a man, and a man to a worm.

AMBROSE BIERCE, 1842-1914?, *The Devil's Dictionary*

I do not live to eat, but eat to live.
Non ut edam vivo, sed ut vivam edo.

QUINTILIAN, *c.* 35-95

One should eat to live and not live to eat.

MOLIERE, 1622-1673, *L'Avare*

He who eats for two must work for three.

KURDISH PROVERB

To eat is human—to stuff is divine.

> MARSHALL EFRON, in television performance
> *The American Dream Machine*, 1971

I look upon it, that he who does not mind his belly
will hardly mind anything else.

> SAMUEL JOHNSON, 1709-1784,
> in James Boswell's *Life*

It is a difficult task, O Citizens, to make speeches to
the belly, which has no ears.

> PLUTARCH, 46?-120?, *Lives*, "Marcus Cato"

Grub first, then ethics.   BERTHOLD BRECHT, 1898-1956

Seeing is deceiving. It's eating that's believing.

> JAMES THURBER, 1894-1961, *Further Fables for Our Times*

He who wants to eat cannot sleep.

> BRILLAT-SAVARIN, 1755-1826, *Physiologie du Goût*

Better beans and bacon in peace than cakes and ale
in fear.   AESOP, *fl.* 550 B.C.

A man should not so much respect what he eateth as
with whom he eateth.   MONTAIGNE, 1533-1592, *Essays*

Let me smile with the wise, and feed with the rich.

> SAMUEL JOHNSON, 1709-1784,
> in James Boswell's *Life*

Eating should be done in silence, lest the windpipe
open before the gullet, and life be in danger.

The Talmud, c. 200

Whatsoever parteth the hoof, and is cloven footed
and cheweth the cud, among the beasts, that shall ye
eat.   *Leviticus* xi, 3, *c.* 700 B.C.

Some [foods] should be eaten before fully ripe, such
as capers, asparagus, sucking-pigs, and pigeons . . .
others at the moment of perfection, such as melons,
most fruit, mutton and beef . . . , others when they
start to decompose, such as medlars, woodcocks, and
especially pheasants; others, finally, after the meth-
ods of art have removed their deleterious qualities,
such as the potato and cassava root.

BRILLAT-SAVARIN, 1755-1826, *Physiologie du Goût*

On the Day of Atonement it is forbidden to eat or
drink; to wash, to anoint one's self, or to fasten the
shoes. Whoever eats food to the size of a large date,
or drinks as much as a mouthful is guilty.

The Talmud, c. 200

Man is the only animal that can remain on friendly
terms with the victims he intends to eat until he
eats them.   SAMUEL BUTLER, 1835-1902, *Notebooks*

I have no doubt that it is part of the destiny of the
human race, in its gradual improvement, to leave off

eating animals, as surely as the savage tribes have left off eating each other when they came in contact with each other.

HENRY DAVID THOREAU, 1817-1862, *Walden*

Tell me what you eat and I will tell you what you are.   BRILLAT-SAVARIN, 1755-1826, *Physiologie du Goût*

Whatever Miss T. eats
Turns into Miss T.

WALTER DE LA MARE, 1873-1956

Lunch kills half Paris, supper the other half.

MONTESQUIEU, 1689-1755, *Variétés*

One cannot think well, love well, sleep well, if one has not dined well.

VIRGINIA WOOLF, 1882-1941, *A Room of One's Own*

Better a dish of herbs where love is, than a stalled ox and hatred therewith.   *Proverbs* xv, 17, *c*. 350 B.C.

The effect of the chemical compounds contained in food upon physiological and mental activities is far from being thoroughly known. Medical opinion on this point is of little value, for no experiments of sufficient duration have been made upon human beings to ascertain the influence of a given diet. There is no doubt that consciousness is affected by the quantity and quality of the food. Those who dare to

dominate and create should not be fed like manual
workers, or like contemplative monks who, in the
solitude of monasteries, endeavour to repress in their
inner self the turmoil of the secular passions. We
have to discover what food is suitable for human
beings vegetating in offices and factories. What
chemical substances could give intelligence, courage,
and alertness to the inhabitants of a new city. The
race will certainly not be improved merely by sup-
plying children and adolescents with a great abun-
dance of milk, cream, and all known vitamins. It
would be most useful to search for new compounds
which, instead of uselessly increasing the size and
weight of the children and the muscles, would bring
about nervous strength and mental agility. Perhaps
some day a scientist will discover how to manufac-
ture great men from ordinary children, in the same
manner that bees transform a common larva into a
queen by the special food which they know how to
prepare. But it is probable that no chemical agent
alone is capable of greatly improving the individual.

ALEXIS CARREL, 1873-1944, *Man the Unknown*

I have known many meat eaters to be far more non-
violent than vegetarians.

MOHANDAS GANDHI, 1869-1948

Food eaten is sundered in three. The thickest stock
thereof becometh excrement, the middling flesh, and
thinnest mind. Water drunk is sundered in three. The

thickest stock thereof becometh the body's water, the middling blood, and the thinnest breath. Meat eaten is sundered in three. The thickest stock thereof becometh bone, the middling marrow, the thinnest speech.   *The Prasna Upanishad, c. 500 B.C.*

I might glorify my bill of fare until I was tired; but after all, the Scotchman would shake his head and say, "Where's your haggis?" and the Fijian would sigh and say, "Where's your missionary?"
                    MARK TWAIN (SAMUEL CLEMENS),
                    1835-1910, *A Tramp Abroad*

Women, melons, and cheese should be chosen by weight.   SPANISH PROVERB

Food without hospitality is medicine.
                    TAMIL PROVERB

Food saves, food destroys; there is no enemy like food.
                    MARATHI PROVERB

Between two kinds of food, both equally
Remote and tempting, first a man might die
Of hunger, ere he could freely choose.
                    JOHN MILTON, 1608-1674, *Paradise Lost*

There is no love sincerer than the love of food.
                    GEORGE BERNARD SHAW,
                    1856-1950, *Man and Superman*

What God gives and what we take,
'Tis a gift for Christ His sake:
Be the meal of beans and pease,
God be thanked for those and these:
Have we flesh, or have we fish,
All are fragments from his dish.

ROBERT HERRICK, 1591-1674, *Noble Numbers*

A depraved taste in food is gratified with that which
disgusts other people: it is a species of disease.

VOLTAIRE, 1694-1778, *Philosophical Dictionary*

Shem was a sham and a low sham and his lowness
creeped out first via foodstuffs.

JAMES JOYCE, 1882-1941, *Finnegan's Wake*

In thirty-six dishes are seventy-two diseases.

PUNJABI PROVERB

We may find in the long run that tinned food is a
deadlier weapon than the machine gun.

GEORGE ORWELL, 1903-1950,
The Road to Wigan Pier

It has been well said that a hungry man is more
interested in four sandwiches than four freedoms.

HENRY CABOT LODGE, JR., 1902-

It is a fact that great eaters of meat are in general
more cruel and ferocious than other men; this obser-

vation holds good in all places and at all times; the
barbarism of the English is well known.

JEAN-JACQUES ROUSSEAU, 1712-1778, *Émile*

If we examine impartially the progress of gastronomy
in England, we shall find that we have not advanced
as far as we think. The last century was distinguished
by a generation of hungry gluttons and inveterate
topers, whose excesses do not sleep with them in the
tomb, but walk the earth, the bluest of all possible
devils, in the stomachs and brains of their nervous,
morbid descendants. If we have abandoned some of
their bad practices, we have lost some of their good
ones: we no longer force our guests to eat more than
they can digest, or to drink till they disappear under
the table; but we have only escaped Charybdis to
founder on Scylla. We add to the business-imposed
late hour of dining the fashionable affectation of
later, and offer to stomachs too fatigued to cope with
boiled mutton ambitious failures of all sorts of in-
congruities. We have added to the number of our
dishes, and have forgotten how to melt butter. We
have let the beef of our people disappear, and have
grown ashamed of roast beef.

THOMAS LOVE PEACOCK, 1785-1866,
Gastronomy and Civilization

We live in an environment whose principal product
is garbage.

RUSSELL BAKER, *New York Times*, Feb. 23, 1968

A calf that associates with a pig will not eat garbage.
                                          HINDU PROVERB

Americans can eat garbage, provided you sprinkle it
liberally with ketchup, mustard, chili sauce, ta-
basco sauce, cayenne pepper, or any other condiment
which destroys the original flavor of the dish.
            HENRY MILLER, 1891-1980, *Remember to Remember*

A month after publication of Rachel Carson's *Silent
Spring* [1962], occurred the famous debate in the
House of Lords, in which Lord Shackleton referred
to "the story of the cannibal in Polynesia who now
no longer allowed his tribe to eat Americans because
their fat is contaminated with chlorinated hydro-
carbons." He was speaking, the noble Lord explained, "purely in the interests of the export trade.
The figure shows that we are rather more edible than
Americans . . . that we have about two parts per
million of DDT in our bodies, whereas the figure for
Americans is about eleven parts per million."
            PAUL BROOKS, *The Intellectual Digest*, June, 1972

Eating People is Wrong.
            MICHAEL FLANDERS, 1922-   , Title of song

If I were a cassowary
On the plains of Timbuctoo,
I would eat a missionary,
Cassock, band, and hymn-book too.
    BISHOP WILBERFORCE, 1805-1873, Ascribed impromptu verse

There are now three projects on foot to serve me up and help people to breast or dark meat, with or without stuffing.

GROVER CLEVELAND, 1837-1908, *Letter to R. W. Gilder*

Cannibals have the same notions of right and wrong that we have. . . . Eating fallen enemies is only an extra ceremonial. The wrong does not consist in eating them, but in killing them.

VOLTAIRE, 1694-1778, Letter to Frederick the Great

The taste of arsenic was so real in my mouth when I described how Emma Bovary was poisoned, that it cost me two indigestions one upon the other—quite real ones, for I vomited my dinner.

GUSTAVE FLAUBERT, 1821-1880, Letter to Hippolyte Taine

She drank prussic acid without any water,
And died like a Duke-and-a-Duchess's Daughter.

REV. R. H. BARHAM, 1788-1845, *The Tragedy*

Little Willie from his mirror
Licked the mercury right off,
Thinking in his childish error,
It would cure the whooping cough.
At the funeral his mother
Smartly said to Mrs. Brown
" 'Twas a chilly day for Willie
When the mercury went down."

ANONYMOUS

"I have no doubt that this man deliberately took poison and he appears to have done so in a most cold-blooded and heartless way," the coroner remarked in summing up.

"This England," *New Statesman*, 1937

I give you bitter pills in sugar coating. The pills are harmless; the poison is in the sugar.

STANISLAUS LEE, *Unkempt Thoughts*, 1962

If he will die from sugar, why kill him with poison?

PASHTO PROVERB

Antidotes are poison.

SHAKESPEARE, 1564-1616, *Timon of Athens*

Never take the antidote before the poison.

LATIN PROVERB

Everyman to his own poison.   AMERICAN PROVERB

One man's meat is another man's poison.

ENGLISH PROVERB

What's one man's poison, signor,
Is another's meat or drink.

BEAUMONT, 1584-1616 & FLETCHER, 1579-1625, *Love's Care*

What is food to one man may be poison to another.

LUCRETIUS, 96?-55 B.C., *De rerum natura* IV

Mithridates, by frequently drinking poison, rendered it impossible for any poison to hurt him. You, Cinna, by always dining on next to nothing, have taken due precaution against ever perishing from hunger.

MARTIAL, *c*. 40-*c*. 102, *Epigrammata* v

Food, one assumes, provides nourishment, but Americans eat it fully aware that small amounts of poison have been added to improve its appearance and delay its putrefaction.   JOHN CAGE, 1912- , *Silence*

Health warning on apricot pit chewing. California health officials say that apricot kernel consumption can lead to cyanide poisoning. Peach and plum pits, even apple seeds, are dangerous.

San Francisco *Chronicle*, September 3, 1972

of DRINKING

THE cordial drop, the morning dram, I sing,
The midday toddy, and the evening sling.
ANONYMOUS, *Baltimore Weekly Magazine*, 1830

What's drinking?
A mere pause from thinking.
LORD BYRON, 1788-1824, *The Deformed Transformed*

To drink is a Christian diversion,
Unknown to the Turk or the Persian.
WILLIAM CONGREVE, 1670-1729, *Way of the World*

Candy is dandy
But liquor is quicker.   OGDEN NASH, 1902-1973

A bumper of good liquor
Will end a contest quicker
Than justice, judge or vicar.
RICHARD B. SHERIDAN, 1751-1816, *The Duenna*

By drinking grog I lost my life;
    So, lest my fate you meet,
Why, never mix your liquor, lads,
    But always drink it neat.
C. DIBDIN, JR., 1768-1833, *Ben, the Boatswain*

All animals are strictly dry,
They sinless live and swiftly die,
But sinful, ginful, rum-soaked men,
Survive for three score years and ten.
ANONYMOUS

When Methodist preachers come down
    A-preaching that drinking is sinful,
I'll wager the rascals a crown
    They always preach best with a skinful.
OLIVER GOLDSMITH, 1728-1774, *She Stoops to Conquer*

Man wants but little drink below,
    But wants that little strong.
O. W. HOLMES, 1809-1894, *Song of Other Days*

Therefore drink! (Ergo bibamus!)
JOHANN WOLFGANG GOETHE,
1749-1832, *Ergo bibamus*, refrain

Now is the time for drinking, now is the time to beat the earth with unfettered foot.

HORACE, 65-8 B.C., *Odes*

It is a bad man who remembers what went on at a drinking bout.   GREEK PROVERB

I fear the man who drinks water
And so remembers what the rest of us said last night.
Greek Anthology

"A little drop" may end in a great fall.
C. H. SPURGEON, 1834-1892, *Ploughman's Talk*

O God, that men should put an enemy in their mouths to steal away their brains.
WILLIAM SHAKESPEARE, 1564-1616, *Othello*

Clothe warm, eat little, drink well, so shalt thou live.   JOHN FLORIO, 1553?-1625, *First Frutes*

It is a miserable job to dig a well while you are thirsty.   PLAUTUS, 254?-184 B.C., *Mostellaria*

If die I must, let me die drinking in an inn.
WALTER MAP (OR MAPES),
c. 1137-1209, *De nugis curialium*

I do not drink more than a sponge.
FRANCOIS RABELAIS, c. 1495-1553, *Gargantua*

Drink to all healths, but drink not thine own.

JOSEPH HALL, 1574-1656, *Virgidemarium*

He that is drunk is gone from home.

THOMAS FULLER, 1608-1661, *Gnomologia*

No man is drunk so long as he can lie on the floor without holding on.

ANONYMOUS

Not drunk is he who from the floor
Can rise alone and still drink more;
But drunk is he who prostrate lies,
Without the power to drink or rise.

THOMAS LOVE PEACOCK, 1785-1866,
The Misfortunes of Elphin

Bacchus hath drowned more men than Neptune.

THOMAS FULLER, 1608-1661, *Gnomologia*

Drunkenness does not produce faults; it discovers them.

CHINESE PROVERB

Beware of the man who does not drink.

ITALIAN PROVERB

If it wasn't for meat and good drink the women might gnaw the sheets.

ENGLISH PROVERB

He that goes to bed thirsty riseth healthy.

ENGLISH PROVERB

There are more old drunkards than old doctors.

FRENCH PROVERB

First the man takes a drink, then the drink takes a drink, then the drink takes the man.

JAPANESE PROVERB

It is only the first bottle that is expensive.

FRENCH PROVERB

When the arm bends the mouth opens.

DANISH PROVERB

When Porson dined with me, I used to keep him within bounds; but I frequently met him at various houses where he got completely drunk. He would not scruple to return to the dining room, after the company had left it, pour into a tumbler the drops remaining in the wine glasses, and drink off the omnium gatherum.

SAMUEL ROGERS, 1763-1855, *Table Talk*

We made the acquaintance of drinks invented by the Creoles during the period of Louey Cans, in which they are still served at the side doors.

O. HENRY, 1862-1910, *Hostages to Momus*

A man who has been drinking wine at all freely should never go into a new company. With those who have partaken of wine with him he may be

pretty well in unison, but he will probably be offensive, or appear ridiculous to other people.

SAMUEL JOHNSON, 1709-1784,
in James Boswell's *Life*

Fermented spirits please our common people because
they banish care and all consideration of future or
present evils.

EDMUND BURKE, 1729-1797, *The Sublime and Beautiful*

I have very poor and unhappy brains for drinking;
I could wish courtesy would invent some other custom for entertainment.

WILLIAM SHAKESPEARE, 1564-1616, *Othello*

I always naturally hated drinking; and yet I have
often drunk, with disgust at the time, attended by
great sickness the next day, only because I then considered drinking as a necessary qualification for a fine
gentleman, and a man of pleasure.

LORD CHESTERFIELD, 1694-1773, Letter to his son

Take that liquor away, I never touch strong drink.
I like it too well to fool with it.

T. J. (STONEWALL) JACKSON, 1824-1863,
On refusing a mint julep

Often Daddy sat up very late working on a case of
Scotch.

ROBERT BENCHLEY, 1889-1945, *Editha's Christmas Burglar*

Drinking when we are not thirsty and making love at all seasons, madam: that is all there is to distinguish us from the other animals.

PIERRE DE BEAUMARCHAIS, 1732-1799, *Le Mariage de Figaro*

Damn temperance and he that first invented it!

CHARLES LAMB, 1775-1834, Letter to Dorothy Wordsworth

Temperate men drink the most, because they drink the longest.   C. C. COLTON, *c.* 1780-1832, *Lacon*

Temperance and labor are the two best physicians of man. Labor sharpens his appetite and temperance prevents him abusing it.

JEAN-JACQUES ROUSSEAU, 1712-1778, *Émile*

"What did the Governor of North Carolina say to the Governor of South Carolina?"
"Excellent notion. It *is* a long time between drinks."

RUDYARD KIPLING, 1865-1936, *The Light that Failed*

o*f* BREAKING FAST

THE morning cup of coffee has an exhilaration about it which the cheering influence of the afternoon or evening cup of tea cannot be expected to reproduce.
OLIVER WENDELL HOLMES, SR., 1809-1894, *Over the Teacups*

Bring porridge, bring sausage, bring fish for a start,
Bring kidneys and mushrooms and partridges' legs,
But let the foundation be bacon and eggs.
A. P. HERBERT, 1890-1971, *A Book of Ballads*

The still hissing bacon and the eggs that looked like tufts of primroses.
BENJAMIN DISRAELI, 1804-1881, *Coningsby*

But since he stood for England
  And knew what England means
Unless you give him bacon
  You must not give him beans.
                    G. K. CHESTERTON, 1874-1936, *The Englishman*

Pig flesh is generally heavy and indigestible, especially for people who don't exercise much. But when
it is hardened with salt and dried with smoke, it is
even more unhealthy. That is bacon. Bacon fat, besides, is usually rancid and acrid, can only have an
evil effect on the stomach, and can excoriate the
mouth and throat. Bacon made from acorn-fattened
pigs is generally firmer, and consequently better,
than from bran-fed animals.
                    ALEXANDRE DUMAS, 1802-1870

We breakfasted at Cullen. They set fried haddocks
along with our tea. I ate one; but Dr. Johnson was
disgusted by the sight of them, so they were removed.
                    JAMES BOSWELL, 1740-1795, *Life of Johnson*

Give good heed to serve eggs of an oblong shape, for
they have a better flavor and are whiter than the
round; they are firm and enclose a male yolk.
                    HORACE, 65-8 B.C., *Satires*

A priest's rule that is true:
Those eggs are best that are
long and white and new.
                    JOHN HARINGTON, 1561-1612, *The Englishman's Doctor*

An egg boiled very soft is not unwholesome.

JANE AUSTEN, 1775-1817, *Emma*

The vulgar boil, the learned roast an egg.

ALEXANDER POPE, 1688-1744,
The Second Book of Horace

Orpheus, Pythagoras, and their sectators—good and humane people as ever lived—unceasingly recommended in their discourses to abstain from eggs, in order not to destroy a germ which nature had destined for the production of chicken. Many allowed themselves to be persuaded, and would have believed it an unpardonable crime if they had eaten a tiny *omelette*, or boiled eggs. Many of the most learned philosophers held eggs in a kind of respect approaching to veneration, because they saw in them the emblem of the world and the four elements. The shell, they said, represented the earth; the white, water; the yolk, fire; and air was found under the shell.

The shepherds had a singular manner of cooking eggs without the aid of fire: they placed them in a sling, which they turned so rapidly that the friction of the air heated them to the exact point required for use.

ALEXIS SOYER, 1809-1858,
A Shilling Cookery for the People

Is there any taste in the white of an egg?

Job vi, 6, 325 B.C.

There is no such thing as a pretty good omelet.
FRENCH PROVERB

He that would have eggs must endure the cackling of hens.   DUTCH PROVERB quoted by ERASMUS, 1466-1536

Tennyson does not like his eggs too lightly cooked. Today at breakfast there was a pretty waitress, and he sent his eggs to be more boiled, and then, in the damsel's native tongue, expostulated with her as to the softness of her eggs and the apparent hardness of her heart. It was very pleasant to hear his grave but gallant remonstrance and her merry laugh. He is delightful.
FREDERICK LOCKER-LAMPSON, 1821-1895, *Memoir of Tennyson*

"I'm afraid you've got a bad egg, Mr. Jones."
"Oh no, my Lord, I assure you! Parts of it are excellent!"   *Punch*, 1895

They are a nutritious food, wholesome in every way, except when boiled too hard; although there are some stomachs which reject them. They can be employed in almost every dish with advantage, and one weighing two ounces contains nearly the same amount of nourishment as an ounce of meat and an ounce of bread; therefore when eggs are eighteen for a shilling, equal to two pounds four ounces, they are not a very dear article of food.
ALEXIS SOYER, 1809-1858, *A Shilling Cookery for the People*

Who can help loving a land that has taught us six hundred and eighty-five ways to dress eggs?

THOMAS MOORE, 1779-1852, *The Fudge Family in Paris*

Every living thing comes from an egg.
Omne vivum ex ovo.

WILLIAM HARVEY, 1578-1657

The egg's . . . a chicken *in potentia*.

BEN JONSON, 1573?-1637, *The Alchemist*

I never see an egg brought on my table but I feel penetrated with the wonderful change it would have undergone but for my gluttony; it might have been a gentle useful hen, leading her chickens with a care and vigilance which speaks shame to many women.

ST. JOHN DE CREVECOEUR, 1735-1813,
Letters from an American Farmer

Better to have an egg today than a hen tomorrow.

ITALIAN PROVERB

A hen is only an egg's way of making another egg.

SAMUEL BUTLER, 1835-1902, *Life and Habit*

Wall Street Lays an Egg!

SIME SILVERMAN, 1873-1933, Headline in *Variety*

You can't unscramble scrambled eggs.

AMERICAN PROVERB

Oh, tough as a steak, was Yukon Jake—
Hard-boiled as a picnic egg.

EDWARD E. PARAMORE, JR., *The Ballad of Yukon Jake*

The roosters lay eggs in Kansas.
The roosters lay eggs as big as beer kegs.
And the hair grows on their legs in Kansas.

ANONYMOUS, Popular Song, *c.* 1880

The noise from good toast should reverberate in the head like the thunder of July. E. V. LUCAS, 1868-1938

What *can* it be, that subtle treachery that lurks in tea-cakes, and is totally absent in the rude honesty of toast? JOHN RUSKIN, 1819-1900

"Why sir, in fact, and to make a long story short, on coming near London, we breakfasted at Baldock. . . . Well, now, sir, would you believe it, though we were quite on regular time, the breakfast was precisely good for nothing?"

"And Wordsworth?"

"He observed—"

"What did he observe?"

"That the buttered toast looked, for all the world, as if it had been soaked in hot water."

THOMAS DE QUINCEY, 1785-1859

I had never had a piece of toast
Particularly long and wide,

But fell upon the sanded floor,
And always on the buttered side.

JAMES PAYNE, 1830-1898

No bread. Then bring me some toast.

Punch, 1852

Shrove Tuesday . . . There is a bell rung, call'd the Pancake-Bell, the sound whereof makes thousands of people distracted, and forgetful either of manners or humanities; then there is a thing call'd wheaten floure, which the cookes do mingle with water, eggs, spice and other magicall enchantments, and then they put it little by little into a frying-pan of boiling suet, where it makes a confused dismall hissing, untill at last by the skill of the Cooke, it is transformed into the form of a Flip-Jack, call'd a Pancake, which ominous incantation, the ignorant people do devoure very greedillie.

JOHN TAYLOR, 1580-1623

Farm hands begin each day by eating three dozen pancakes. H. L. MENCKEN, 1880-1956 &

GEORGE JEAN NATHAN, 1882-1958, *The American Credo*

I can only get along by eating no meat, especially as I have had a lot of oat-cakes given me: which monopolizes my breakfasts, I adore oat-cakes: yet I was glad to have eaten the last one this morning.

ARNOLD BENNETT, 1867-1931, *Letters to his Nephew*

Oats: A grain which in England is generally given to horses, but in Scotland supports the people.

SAMUEL JOHNSON, 1709-1784, *Dictionary*

It is not the horse that draws the cart, but the oats.

RUSSIAN PROVERB

My little Jennie [Mrs. Carlyle] was in hands with the marmalade that day: none ever made such marmalade for me, pure as liquid amber, in taste and in look almost poetically delicate, and it was the only one of her pretty and industrious confitures that I individually cared for; which made her doubly diligent and punctual about it.

THOMAS CARLYLE, 1795-1881, *Reminiscenses*

Honey is too good for a bear.

THOMAS FULLER, 1608-1661, *Gnomologia*

My son, eat thou honey, because it is good.

Proverbs xxiv, 13

Honey is one of the best of our high energy producing foods, because it is composed almost entirely of simple sugars which are easily assimilated. Because of this, honey is a valuable food where normal digestive activities have been impaired by disease or old age. It is also recognized as a highly suitable food for babies and children.

Old Farmer's Almanac, 1932

Hast thou found honey? Eat so much as is convenient for thee.   HEBREW PROVERB

Milk is a kind of prescription which a cow makes up for her calf, inside her own body, and like all other chemists she never makes it up quite the same twice together.   SAMUEL BUTLER, 1835-1902, *Note Books*

Milk: That delightful substance which comes out of the wonderful chemistry which God has given the cow for the delight of the world and the sustenance of children.
                CHAUNCEY DEPEW, 1834-1928, Speech in the Senate

The cow is of the bovine ilk;
One end is moo, the other, milk.
                        OGDEN NASH, 1900-1973, *The Cow*

A red cow gives good milk.   ENGLISH PROVERB

It's by the mouth o' the cow that milk comes.
                                        SCOTTISH PROVERB

Milk . . . causeth the body to wax gross, and for amending of a dry constitution, and for them that are attenuated by long sickness, or are in a consumption, it is by reason of the excellent moistening, cooling and nourishing faculty of it, of singular efficacy.
                        TOBIAS VENNER, 1577 -1660,
                        Via recta ad vitam longam

Milk before wine
I would 'twere mine;
Milk taken after,
Is poison's daughter.

OLD ENGLISH BALLAD

Drinka pinta milka day.

ADVERTISING SLOGAN, 20th Century

Cream . . . is the very head and flour of milk: but is somewhat of a gross nourishment, and by reason of the unctuosity of it, quickly cloyeth the stomach, relaxeth and weakeneth the retentive faculty thereof, and is easily converted into phlegm, and vaporous fumes.   TOBIAS VENNER, 1577-1660, *Via recta ad vitam longam*

Yoghurt is very good for the stomach, the lumbar regions, appendicitis and apotheosis.

EUGENE IONESCO, 1912- , *The Bald Prima Donna*

o*f* SNACKS
& REFRESHMENTS

FRITZ, at the center table mincing shallots, gave me a look and spoke, "That is an insult, I pull your nose. My shad roe *aux fines herbes* is a dish for a king." . . . "You may have to invent a dish for a king made of peanut butter." . . . "Not impossible, Archie. The problem would be to crack the oil. Not vinegar; it would take too much. Perhaps lime juice, with or without a drop or two of onion juice. I'll try it tomorrow." REX STOUT, 1886-1975, *Too Many Clients*

My favorite sandwich is peanut butter, baloney, cheddar cheese, lettuce and mayonnaise on toasted bread with catsup on the side.

SENATOR HUBERT HUMPHREY, 1911-1978

Course, we don't get meat as often as our forefathers but we have our peanut butter and radio.

WILL ROGERS, 1879-1935, *Autobiography*

I doubt whether the world holds for any one a more soul-stirring surprise than the first adventure with ice-cream.

HEYWOOD BROUN, 1888-1939, *Seeing Things at Night*

You'll get pie in the sky when you die.

JOE HILL as quoted by Alan Lomax

If one begins eating peanuts one cannot stop.

H. L. MENCKEN, 1880-1956 & GEORGE JEAN NATHAN, 1882-1958, *The American Credo*

I hate television. I hate it as much as peanuts. But I can't stop eating peanuts.

ORSON WELLES, 1915-   , in *New York Herald Tribune*

In Venice every holiday has its appropriate viand. During carnival all the butter and cheese shop-windows are whitened with the snow of beatened cream—*panamontata*. At San Marino the bakers parade troops of gingerbread warriors. Later, for Christmas, comes *mandorlato*, which is a candy made of honey and enriched with almonds. In its season only can any of these devotional delicacies be had; but there is a species of cruller, fried in oil, which has all seasons for its own. On the occasion of every *festa*, and every *sagra* (which is the holiday of one parish only), stalls are erected in the squares for the cooking and sale of these crullers, between which and the religious sentiment proper to the whole year there seems to be some occult relation.

In the winter the whole city seems to abandon herself to cooking for the public, till she threatens to hopelessly disorder the law of demand and supply. There are, to begin with, the caffé and restaurants of every class. Then there are the cook-shops, and the poulterers', and the sausagemakers'. Then, also, every fruit-stall is misty and odorous with roast apples, boiled beans, cabbage, and potatoes. The chestnut-roasters infest every corner, and men, women, and children cry roast pumpkin at every turn—till, at last, hunger seems an absurd and foolish vice, and the ubiquitous beggars, no less than the habitual abstemiousness of every class of the population, become the most perplexing and maddening of anomalies. WILLIAM DEAN HOWELLS, 1837-1920, *Venetian Life*

Almonds come to those who have no teeth.
CHINESE PROVERB

Heaven gives almonds to those who have no teeth.
H. W. LONGFELLOW, 1807-1882,
The Spanish Student

Don't eat too many almonds; they add weight to the breasts. COLETTE, 1873-1954, *Gigi*

# of BEVERAGES

TEA! thou soft, thou sober, sage, and venerable liquid, thou female tongue-running, smile-soothing, heart-opening, wink-tippling cordial, to whose glorious insipidity I owe the happiest moments of my life, let me fall prostrate.

COLLEY CIBBER, 1671-1757, *The Lady's Last Stake*

Tea: The cups that cheer but not inebriate.

WILLIAM COWPER, 1731-1800, *The Task*

Tea: The infusion of a China plant sweetened with the pith of an Indian cane.

JOSEPH ADDISON, 1672-1719, *The Spectator*, No. 69

Tea possesses an acrid astringent quality, peculiar to most leaves and exterior bark of trees, and corrodes and paralyzes the nerves.

JESSEY TORREY, *The Moral Instructor*, 1819

Polly, put the kettle on,
And let's drink tea.   NURSERY RHYME, *c.* 1750

Thank God for tea! What would the world do without tea! How did it exist? I am glad I was not born before tea!   SYDNEY SMITH, 1771-1845, *Memoir*

Indeed, Madam, your ladyship is very sparing of your tea: I protest the last I took was no more than water bewitched.   JONATHAN SWIFT, 1667-1745,
Polite Conversations

The hot water is to remain upon it no longer than whiles you can say the Miserere Psalm very leisurely.

SIR KENELM DIGBY, 1603-1665

My tea was so good and my cups so large that they always used to say: "We'll have tea at Haydon's in the grand style."

BENJAMIN ROBERT HAYDON, 1786-1846, *Life*

"What are you—a sorcerer?"
"Only at home. In company I drink out of a cup."

FRANK MUIR AND DENNIS MORGAN,
in *Take It from Here*, B.B.C. Comedy Series

Love and scandal are the best sweeteners of tea.
HENRY FIELDING, 1707-1754,
Love in Several Masques

Don't pour out tea before putting sugar in the cup, or some one will be drowned.
AMERICAN NEGRO PROVERB

The slavery of the tea and coffee and other slop kettle.
WILLIAM COBBETT, 1762-1835, Advice to Young Men

Look here, Steward, if this is coffee, I want tea; but if this is tea, then I wish for coffee.   Punch, 1902

Coffee has two virtues: it is wet and warm.
DUTCH PROVERB

Coffee, though a useful medicine, if drunk constantly will at length induce a decay of health, and hectic fever.   JESSE TORREY, The Moral Instructor, 1819

Coffee should be black as Hell, strong as death, and sweet as love.   TURKISH PROVERB

Coffee:
Black as the devil,
Hot as hell,
Pure as an angel,
Sweet as love.
CHARLES MAURICE DE TALLEYRAND, 1754-1838

Coffee: Induces wit. Good only if it comes through Havre. After a big dinner party it is taken standing up. Take it without sugar—very swank: gives the impression you have lived in the East.

GUSTAVE FLAUBERT, 1821-1880, *Dictionnaire des Idées Reçu*

You can tell when you have crossed the frontier into Germany because of the badness of the coffee.

EDWARD VII, 1841-1910

Why do they always put mud into coffee on board steamers?

W. M. THACKERAY, 1811-1863, *The Kicklebury's on the Rhine*

Coffee from the top of the cup, chocolate from the bottom.   VENETIAN PROVERB

The superiority of chocolate, both for health and nourishment, will soon give it the same preference over tea and coffee in America which it has in Spain.

THOMAS JEFFERSON, 1743-1826, Letter to John Adams

On the 16 of July (1858) for the first time in his life that distinguished critic and poet (A. H. Clough) tasted Soda Water, and it is the first American institution on which I have heard him bestow unqualified praise. He is not quite sure, however, that it will do in the long run, and seems to have some vague notion that chemicals, however refreshing for the moment, must corrode the vitals.

CHARLES ELIOT NORTON, 1827-1908, *Letters*

The American millionairess Barbara Hutton, the
Princess de Champacak, drinks more than twenty
bottles of Coca-Cola each day. *Women's Wear Daily*, 1971

Cola drinks used to be liberally laced with cocaine
but Coca Cola no longer contains the "real thing"
which originally gave the drink its name.
   Today cocaine has been replaced in cola drinks by
another stimulant, caffeine. A 16-ounce bottle of cola
contains a bit more caffeine than would be found in a
cup of coffee. Drinking too much cola near bedtime
might cause insomnia.
DOCTOR HIP POCRATES, San Francisco *Chronicle*, September 3, 1972

Water is the best of all things.
                              PINDAR, 522?-443 B.C., *Olympian Odes*

The natural, temperate and necessary beverage for
the thirsty is water.
               CLEMENT OF ALEXANDRIA, A.D. 150?-220?, *Paedagogus*

Water . . . doth very greatly deject the appetite, destroy the natural heat, and overthrow the strength
of the stomach, and consequently, confounding the
concoction, it is the cause of crudities, fluctuations,
and windiness in the body.
               TOBIAS VENNER, 1577-1660, *Via recta ad vitam longam*

The greatest necessity of the soldier is water.
                              NAPOLEON I, 1769-1821

Water, water, everywhere,
Nor any drop to drink.

SAMUEL TAYLOR COLERIDGE,
1772-1834, *The Ancient Mariner*

While this water fills my cup,
    Duns dare not assail me;
Sheriffs shall not lock me up,
    Nor my neighbors bail me.

JOHN PIERPONT, 1785-1866, *Airs of Palestine*

Water is the only drink for a wise man.

HENRY DAVID THOREAU, 1817-1862, *Walden*

Drinking water neither makes a man sick, nor in
debt, nor his wife a widow.

H. G. BOHN, 1796-1884, *Handbook of Proverbs*

Water taken in moderation cannot hurt anybody.

MARK TWAIN, 1835-1910, *Notebook*

All sinners are water drinkers; it is well-proven by
the Deluge.   COMTE DE SEGUR,
1753-1820, *Chanson Morale*

No poems can please long, nor live, which are written by water drinkers.   HORACE, 65-27 B.C.

Water is insipid, inodorous, colorless, and smooth;
it is found, when not cold, to be a great resolver of

spasms, and lubricator of the fibers; this power it probably owes to its smoothness.

EDMUND BURKE, 1729-1797, *The Sublime and the Beautiful*

Dip in the river who loves water.

WILLIAM BLAKE, 1757-1827, *The Marriage of Heaven and Hell*

Full many a man, both young and old
　Is brought to his sarcophagus
By pouring water, icy cold,
　Down his warm esophagus.

ANONYMOUS

And if from man's vile arts I flee
And drink pure water from the pump,
I gulp down infusoria
And quarts of raw bacteria,
And hideous rotatorae,
And slimy diatomacae
And various animalculae
Of middle, high and low degree.

WILLIAM JUNIPER, *The True Drunkard's Delight*, 1933

It's all right to drink like a fish—if you drink what a fish drinks.

MARY PETTIBONE POOLE, *A Glass Eye at the Keyhole*, 1938

o∮ APPETITE

Appetite comes by eating.

FRANCOIS RABELAIS, c. 1495-1553, *Gargantua*

A man's palate can, in time, become accustomed to anything. NAPOLEON I, 1769-1821

New meat begets a new appetite.

JOHN RAY, 1627-1705, *English Proverbs*

He who would not lose his appetite should not go into the kitchen. GERMAN PROVERB

An eating-house keeper doesn't care how big your appetite is. CHINESE PROVERB

All things require skill but an appetite.

GEORGE HERBERT, 1593-1633, *Outlandish Proverbs*

That which is not good is not delicious
To a well-governed and wise appetite.

JOHN MILTON, 1608-1674, *Comus*

'Tis not the meat, but 'tis the appetite
Makes eating a delight.

SIR JOHN SUCKLING, 1609-1642, *Of Thee, Kind Boy*

The poor seek food, the rich seek an appetite.

HINDI PROVERB

Poor men seek meat for their stomach; rich men
stomach for their meat.

THOMAS FULLER, 1608-1661, *Gnomology*

Things taste better in small houses.

QUEEN VICTORIA, 1819-1901

Now good digestion wait on appetite,
And health on both!

WILLIAM SHAKESPEARE, 1564-1616, *Macbeth*

Let appetite obey reason.

CICERO, 106-43 B.C., *De officiis*

Leave with an appetite.

WILLIAM BULLEIN, *The Government of Health*, 1558

If thou rise with an appetite thou art sure never to sit down without one.

WILLIAM PENN, 1644-1718, *Fruits of Solitude*

Who rises from a feast
With that keen appetite with which he sits down?

WILLIAM SHAKESPEARE, 1564-1616, *The Merchant of Venice*

Does not the appetite alter? A man loves the meat in his youth that he cannot endure in his age.

WILLIAM SHAKESPEARE, 1564-1616, *Much Ado About Nothing*

The appetites of the belly and the palate, far from diminishing as men grow older, go on increasing.

CICERO, 106-43 B.C., *Ad Caelium*

Put a knife to thy throat if thou be a man given to appetite.   *Proverbs* xxiii, 2, *c.* 350 B.C.

o*f* APPETIZERS

THE olive tree is surely the richest gift of Heaven. I can scarcely except bread.

THOMAS JEFFERSON, 1743-1826, Letter to George Wythe

There is an Italian sauce called *caviaro*, which begins to be in use with us, such vain affectors are we of novelties. It is prepared of the spawn of the sturgeon: the very name doth well express its nature, that it is good to beware of it.

TOBIAS VENNER, 1577-1660, *Via recta ad vitam longam*

There is more simplicity in a man who eats caviar on impulse than in a man who eats Grapenuts on principle.

G. K. CHESTERTON, 1874-1936

Anchova's, the famous meat of drunkards, and of
them that desire to have their drinke, oblectate the
pallat, doe nourish nothing at all, but a naughty
cholericke blood . . . and are therefore chiefly profitable for vintners.

TOBIAS VENNER, 1577-1660, *Via recta ad vitam longam*

My idea of heaven is, eating *pâtés de foie gras* to the
sound of trumpets.   SYDNEY SMITH, 1771-1845

The Ritz Hotel sent me some *pâté de foie gras* yesterday. This means *pâté de foie gras* at every meal as the
stuff won't keep.

ARNOLD BENNETT, 1867-1931, Letter to his Nephew

Cocktail is a stimulating liquor, composed of spirits
of any kind, sugar, water, and bitters.

ANONYMOUS, *New York Balance*, May 13, 1806

Cocktail:
A little whisky to make it strong,
A little water to make it weak,
A little lemon to make it sour,
A little sugar to make it sweet.   ANONYMOUS

The cocktail is a pleasant drink;
It's mild and harmless I don't think,
When you've had one you call for two,
And then you don't care what you do.

GEORGE ADE, 1866-1944, *The Sultan of Sulu*

Chilled Martini like Ithuriel's spear
Transfixing all dubiety within,
Oiled by an olive and shred of lemon peel.

WILLIAM ROSE BENET, 1886-1950

Cocktails have all the disagreeability without the utility of a disinfectant.

SHANE LESLIE, in the *London Observer*, 1939

A cocktail is to a glass of wine as rape is to love.

PAUL CLAUDEL, 1868-1955

The cocktail party has the form of friendship without the warmth and devotion. It is the device for getting rid of social obligations hurriedly en masse, or making overtures toward more serious social relationships, as in the etiquette of whoring.

BROOKS ATKINSON, 1894-1984, *Once Around the Sun*

o∫ DINING

THAT all-softening overpowering knell,
The tocsin of the soul,—the dinner bell.

LORD BYRON, 1788-1824, Don Juan

Heavenly Father, bless us,
   And keep us all alive,
There's ten of us to dinner
   And not enough for five.

ANONYMOUS, Hodge's Grace, c. 1850

The family that dines the latest
Is in our street esteemed the greatest.

HENRY FIELDING, 1701-1754, Letter to Robert Walpole

The usual dinner-hour is two o'clock. A dinner party takes place at five; and at an evening party, they seldom sup later than eleven; so that it goes hard but one gets home, even from a rout, by midnight. I never could find out any difference between a party at Boston and a party in London, saving at the former place all assemblies are held at more rational hours; that the conversation may possibly be a little louder and more cheerful; that a guest is usually expected to ascend to the very top of the house to take his cloak off; that he is certain to see, at every dinner, an unusual amount of poultry on the table; and at every supper, at least two mighty bowls of hot stewed oysters, in any one of which a half-grown Duke of Clarence might be smothered easily. At eight o'clock, the shelves being taken down and put away and the tables joined together, everybody sat down to the tea, coffee, bread, butter, salmon, shad, liver, steak, potatoes, pickles, ham, chops, black-puddings, and sausages, all over again. Some were fond of compounding this variety, and having it all on their plates at once. As each gentleman got through his own personal amount of tea, coffee, bread, butter, salmon, shad, liver, steak, potatoes, pickles, ham, chops, black-puddings, and sausages, he rose up and walked off. When everybody had done with everything, the fragments were cleared away: and one of the waiters appearing anew in the character of a barber, shaved such of the company as desired to be shaved; while the remainder looked on,

or yawned over their newspapers. Dinner was breakfast again, without the tea and coffee; supper and
breakfast were identical.

CHARLES DICKENS, 1812-1870, *American Notes*

At table, I prefer the witty before the grave; in bed,
beauty before goodness; and in common discourse,
eloquence, whether or no there be sincerity.

MICHEL DE MONTAIGNE, 1533-1595, *Essays*

A man seldom thinks with more earnestness of anything than he does of his dinner.

SAMUEL JOHNSON, 1709-1784

Music with dinner is an insult both to the cook and
the violinist.   G. K. CHESTERTON, 1874-1936

Everything ends this way in France—everything.
Weddings, christenings, duels, burials, swindlings,
diplomatic affairs—everything is a pretext for a good
dinner.   JEAN ANOUILH, 1910-   , *Cécile*

We should look for someone to eat and drink with
before looking for something to eat and drink, for
dining alone is leading the life of a lion or wolf.

EPICURUS, 342?-270 B.C., *Aphorisms*

Oh, the pleasure of eating my dinner alone!

CHARLES LAMB, 1775-1834,
Letter to Mrs. Wordsworth

Your supper is like the Hidalgo's dinner; very little meat, and a great deal of tablecloth.

H. W. LONGFELLOW, 1807-1882,
The Spanish Student

And I will profess for myself and other Englishmen, passing through Italy so famous for temperance, that we often observed, that howsoever we might have a pullet and some flesh prepared for us, eating it with a moderate proportion of bread, the Italians at the same time, with a charger full of herbs for a salad, and with roots, and like meats of small price, would each of them eat two or three penny-worth of bread. And since all fullness is ill, and that of bread worst, I think we were more temperate in our diet, though eating more flesh, than they eating so much more bread than we did. It is true that the English prepare largely for ordinary diet for themselves and their friends coming by chance, and at feasts for invited friends are so excessive in the number of dishes, as the table is not thought well-furnished, except they stand one upon another. Neither used they to set drink on the table, for which no room is left, but the cups and glasses served in upon a side table, drink being offered to none, till they call for it.

FYNES MORYSON, 1566-1630, *Itinerary*

No Roman was ever able to say, "I dined last night with the Borgias."

MAX BEERBOHM, 1872-1956, *Hosts and Guests*

Yesterday I dined with Alfred Tennyson at the Cock
Tavern, Temple Bar. We had two chops, one pickle,
two cheeses, one pint of stout, one pint of port, and
three cigars.   RICHARD MONCKTON MILES, 1809-1885

The Wordsworths never dine . . . they hate such
doings; when they are hungry they go to the cup-
board and eat . . . Mr. Wordsworth will live for a
whole month on cold beef, and next on cold bacon.
          MRS. HOLLAND, 1770-1845, Letter to Miss Mitford

Thackeray settled like a meat-fly on whatever one
had for dinner, and made one sick of it.
                    JOHN RUSKIN, 1819-1900, *Fors Clavigera*

His dinner is his other work, for he sweats at it as
much as at labor; he is a terrible fastener on a piece
of beef, and you may have hope to stave the guard
off sooner.   JOHN EARLE, 1601?-1665, *Microcosmographia*

Home to dinner, and there I took occasion, from
the blackness of the meat as it came out of the pot,
to fall out with my wife and my maid for their
sluttery, and so left the table, and went up to read
in Mr. Selden's till church time, and then my wife
and I to church.   SAMUEL PEPYS, 163-31703, *Diary*

My wife had got ready a very fine dinner—*viz.*, a
dish of marrow-bones; a leg of mutton; a loin of
veal; a dish of fowl; three pullets and two dozen of

larks all in a dish; a great tart, a neat's tongue, a
dish of anchovies, a dish of prawns and cheese.

SAMUEL PEPYS, 1633-1703, *Diary*

Home, and, being washing-day, dined upon cold
meat.   SAMUEL PEPYS, 1633-1703, *Diary*

Great and late suppers are very offensive to the whole
body, especially to the head and eyes, by reason of
the multitude of vapors that ascend from the meats
that have been plentifully received.

TOBIAS VENNER, 1577-1660, *Via recta ad vitam longam*

In our private room the cloth could not, for any
earthly consideration, have been laid for dinner without a huge glass dish of cranberries in the middle of
the table; and breakfast would have been no breakfast unless the principal dish were a deformed beef-
steak with a great flat bone in the centre, swimming
in hot butter, and sprinkled with the very blackest
of all possible pepper.

We are to be on *The Messenger* three days; arriving at
Cincinnati (barring accidents) on Monday morning.
There are three meals a day. Breakfast at seven, dinner at half-past twelve, supper about six. At each,
there are a great many small dishes and plates upon
the table, with very little in them; so that although
there is every appearance of a mighty "spread,"
there is seldom really more than a joint: except for

those who fancy slices of beetroot, shreds of dried beef, complicated entanglements of yellow pickle; maize, Indian corn, apple-sauce and pumpkin.

Some people fancy all these little dainties together (and sweet preserves beside), by way of relish to their roast pig. They are generally those dyspepsic ladies and gentlemen who eat unheard-of quantities of hot corn (almost as good for the digestion as a kneaded pin-cushion), for breakfast, and for supper. Those who do not observe this custom, and those who help themselves several times instead, usually suck their knives and forks meditatively, until they have decided what to take next: then pull them out of their mouths; put them in a dish; help themsleves; and fall to work again. At dinner there is nothing to drink upon the table, but great jugs full of cold water. Nobody says anything at any meal, to anybody. All the passengers are very dismal, and seem to have tremendous secrets weighing on their minds. There is no conversation, no laughter, no cheerfulness, no sociality, except in spitting; and that is done in silent fellowship round the stove, when the meal is over. Every man sits down, dull and languid: swallows his fare as if breakfasts, dinners and suppers, were necessities of nature never to be coupled with recreation or enjoyment; and having bolted his food in a gloomy silence, bolts himself in the same state. But for these animal observances, you might suppose the whole male portion of the company to be the melancholy ghosts of departed bookkeepers,

who had fallen dead at the desk; such is their weary
air of business and calculation. Undertakers on duty
would be sprightly beside them; and a collation of
funeral baked meats, in comparison with these
meals, would be sparkling festivity.

CHARLES DICKENS, 1812-1870, American Notes

A warmed-up dinner was never worth anything.

NICOLAS BOILEAU, 1636-1711, Le Lutrin

This was a good dinner enough, to be sure, but it
was not a dinner to ask a man to.

SAMUEL JOHNSON, 1709-1784

My Dinner was brought, and Four Persons of Quality, whom I remember to have seen very near the
King's Person, did me the Honour to dine with me.
We had two Courses, of three Dishes each. In the
first Course, there was a Shoulder of Mutton, cut
into an Aequilateral Triangle, a piece of Beef into a
Rhomboides, and a Pudding into a Cycloid. The
second Course was two ducks, trussed up into the
Form of Fiddles; Sausages and Puddings resembling
flutes and Haut-boys, and a Breast of Veal in the
shape of a Harp. The Servants cut our Bread into
Cones, Cylinders, Parallelograms, and several other
Mathematical Figures.

JONATHAN SWIFT, 1667-1745, Gulliver's Travels

When I demanded of my friend what viands he
  preferred,

He quoth: "A large cold bottle, and a small hot
  bird!"
                EUGENE FIELD, 1850-1895, *The Bottle and the Bird*

The hungry judges soon the sentence sign,
And wretches hang, that jurymen may dine.
                ALEXANDER POPE, 1688-1744, *The Rape of the Lock*

Strange to see how a good dinner and feasting re-
conciles everybody.   SAMUEL PEPYS, 1633-1703, *Diary*

Even the great Napoleon could not eat his dinner
twice.   ALPHONSE KARR, 1808-1890, *Le chemin le plus court*

Serenely full, the epicure would say,
Fate cannot harm me, I have dined today.
                SYDNEY SMITH, 1771-1845

All human history attests
That happiness for man,—the hungry sinner!—
Since Eve ate apples, much depends on dinner.
                LORD BYRON, 1788-1824, *Don Juan*

# of DINING OUT

WE five-to-ten-pound-a-weekers aren't well served in the way of eating-places in London. If your idea of the amount on a meal is one and threepence, it's either Lyons, the Express Dairy, or the A.B.C., or else it's the kind of funeral snack they serve you in the saloon bar, a pint of bitter and a slab of cold pie, so cold that it's colder than the beer. . . . Behind the bright red counter a girl in a tall white cap was fiddling with an ice-box, and somewhere at the back a radio was playing plonk-tiddle-tiddle-plonk, a kind of tinny sound. Why the hell am I coming here? I thought to myself as I went in. There's a kind of atmosphere about these places that gets me down. Everything slick and shiny and stream-lined; mir-

rors, enamel and chromium plate whichever direction you look in. Everything spent on decorations
and nothing on food. No real food at all. Just lists
of stuff with American names, sort of phantom stuff
that you can't taste and can hardly believe in the
existence of. Everything comes out of a carton or a
tin, or is hauled out of a refrigerator or squirted out
of a tap or squeezed out of a tube. No comfort, no
privacy. Tall stools to sit on, a kind of narrow ledge
to eat off, mirrors all around you.

GEORGE ORWELL, 1903-1950, *Coming Up for Air*

There was an hotel in this place, which, like all
hotels in America, had its large dining-room for the
public table. It was an odd, shambling, low-roofed
out-house, half-cowshed and half-kitchen, with a
coarse brown canvas tablecloth, and tin sconces
stuck against the walls, to hold candles at supper-
time. The horseman had gone forward to have coffee
and some eatables prepared, and they were by this
time nearly ready. He had ordered "wheat-bread and
chicken fixings," in preference to "corn-bread and
common doings." The latter kind of refection in-
cludes only pork and bacon. The former compre-
hends broiled ham, sausages, veal cutlets, steaks, and
such other viands of that nature as may be sup-
posed, by a tolerably wide poetical construction, to
"fix" a chicken comfortably in the digestive organs
of any lady or gentleman.

CHARLES DICKENS, 1812-1870, *American Notes*

As one descends in the scale of the restaurants, the
difference is not so noticeable in the prices of the
same dishes, as in the substitution of the cheaper
varieties of food. At the best eating-houses, the Gal-
lic traditions bear sway more or less, but in the poor-
er sort the cooking is done entirely by native artists,
deriving their inspirations from the unsophisticated
tastes of exclusively native diners. It is perhaps
needless to say that they become characteristic and
picturesque as they grow dirty and cheap, until at
last the cookshop perfects the descent with a
triumph of raciness and local coloring. The cook-
shop in Venice opens upon you at almost every turn,
—everywhere, in fact, but in the Piazza and Merceria
—and looking in, you see its vast heaps of frying
fish, and its huge caldrons of ever-boiling broth
which smell to heaven with garlic and onions. In the
seducing windows smoke golden mountains of *polenta* (a thicker kind of mush or hasty-pudding, made
of Indian meal, and universally eaten in North
Italy), platters of crisp minnows, bowls of rice,
roast poultry, dishes of snails and liver; and around
the fascinating walls hang huge plates of bronzed
earthenware for a lavish and a hospitable show, and
for the representation of those scenes of Venetian
story which are modeled upon them in bas-relief.
Here I like to take my unknown friend—my scoun-
drel facchino or rascal gondolier—as he comes to
buy his dinner, and bargains eloquently with the
cook, who stands with a huge ladle in his hand

capable of skimming mysterious things from vasty
depths. I am spellbound by the drama which ensues,
and in which all the chords of the human heart are
touched, from those that tremble at high tragedy, to
those that are shaken by broad farce. When the diner
has bought his dinner, and issues forth with his
polenta in one hand, and his fried minnows or stewed
snails in the other, my fancy fondly follows him to
his gondola-station, where he eats it, and quarrels
volubly with other gondoliers across the Grand
Canal.

A simpler and less ambitious sort of cook-shop
abounds in the region of Rialto, where on market
mornings I have seen it driving a prodigious business
with peasants, gondoliers, and laborers. Its more
limited resources consist chiefly of fried eels, fish,
polenta, and *sguassetto*. The latter is a true *roba vene-
ziana*, and is a loud-flavored broth, made of those
desperate scraps of meat which are found impractical
even by the sausage makers. Another, but more delicate dish, peculiar to the place, is the clotted blood
of poultry, fried in slices with onions. A great number of the families of the poor breakfast at these shops
very abundantly, for three soldi each person.

WILLIAM DEAN HOWELLS, 1837-1920, *Venetian Life*

I had been wrong; Mr. Duncan Hines had been there
before me, as his discreetly beckoning little tin sign
now reassured me. Thunder Bay had at last made the
grade; one could now dine in the certified knowledge

that Duncan approved. I could visualize this ubiquitous little man—his bib full of gravy stains, his pockets full of pills, his soul full of hope—gnawing his way across a continent, leaving diplomas in his wake like a sort of gastronomic Kilroy. I sighed and moved into the hotel. "Peptic ulcers can now be gaily faced," I thought. "Duncan has et here."

ROBERT TRAVERS, *Anatomy of a Murder*, 1958

The road to eminence lies through the cheap and exceedingly uninviting eating-house.

CHINESE PROVERB

If a waiter in a restaurant has a grudge against one he will surreptitiously spit into one's food.

H. L. MENCKEN, 1880-1956 &
GEORGE JEAN NATHAN, 1882-1958, *The American Credo*

By the way, in many jokes the impudence of the waiters in Jewish restaurants is illustrated. Here is an example. A guest calls the waiter, after he has been served, and says, "Look, what's wrong with this chicken you brought me? The one leg is much shorter than the other?" The waiter replies: "Are you eating the chicken or dancing with it?"

THEODORE REIK, *Jewish Wit*, 1962

Never eat in any place called "Mom's."

NELSON ALGREN, 1909-1981

There are all kinds of explanations for the term 86. It almost certainly springs from the argot of waiters, and farther back from the Australians who brought rhyming slang here in the days after the Gold Rush. Eighty-six, said by a cook in reply to a waiter's order means Nix—"We're out of it." By extension it came to mean a man who, by his manners or his lack of funds, was not to be served.

Other bits of old-time waiter's slang involving numbers are: Thirteen, white bread, and also, The boss is around; and eighty-seven and a half, vanilla, for There's a nice looking girl out in front.

CHARLES MC CABE, San Francisco *Chronicle*, June 26, 1972

o∫ BREAD & BUTTER

GIVE us this day our daily bread.   *Matthew vi, 11*

Here is *bread, which strengthens man's heart*, and therefore is called *the staff of life*.
    MATTHEW HENRY, 1662-1714, *Commentaries on the Psalms*

Bread is the staff of life; in which is contained inclusive, the quintessence of beef, mutton, veal, venison, partridge, plum-pudding, and custard: and to render all complete, there is intermingled a due quantity of water, whose crudities are also corrected by yeast or barm, through which means it becomes a wholesome fermented liquor, diffused through the mass of bread.   JONATHAN SWIFT, 1667-1745

Why has our poetry eschewed
The rapture and response of food?
What hymns are sung and praises said
For the home-made miracle of bread?

LOUIS UNTERMEYER, 1885-1977

It was a common saying among the Puritans,
"Brown bread and the Gospel is good fare."

MATHEW CAREY, 1662-1745, *Commentaries*

Upon this island of cheese grows great plenty of
corn, the ears of which produce loaves of bread,
ready made.

RUDOLF RASPE, 1737-1794, *Travels of Baron Munchausen*

In Paris today millions of pounds of bread are sold
daily, made during the previous night by those
strange, half-naked beings one glimpses through cellar windows, whose wild-seeming cries floating out
of those depths always makes a painful impression.
In the morning, one sees these pale men, still white
with flour, carrying a loaf under one arm, going off
to rest and gather new strength to renew their hard
and useful labor when night comes again. I have
always highly esteemed the brave and humble workers who labor all night to produce those soft but
crusty little loaves that look more like cake than
bread.

ALEXANDRE DUMAS, 1802-1870

The bread which I strongly recommend for the labouring class, or those who shall get their bread by "the sweat of their brow," is that made from unbolted flour, or whole meal. It is only the effeminate and delicate that should partake of fine flour. The mass of bread is increased one fifth, and the price lowered, between the difference of the price of bran as flour, or as fodder for cattle.

ALEXIS SOYER, 1809-1858, *A Shilling Cookery for the People*

Bread made only of the branny part of the meal, which the poorest sort of people use, especially in time of dearth and necessity, giveth a very and excremental sort of nourishment to the body; it is well called *panis canicarius*, because it is more fit for dogs than men.

TOBIAS VENNER, 1577-1660, *Via recta ad vitam longam*

The separation of the bran from the flour by bolting, is a matter of luxury, and injurious rather than beneficial as regards the nutritive power of the bread.

J. F. LIEBIG, 1803-1873

You can travel fifty thousand miles in America without once tasting a piece of good bread.

HENRY MILLER, 1891-1980, *Remember to Remember*

Man doth not live by bread alone.

Deuteronomy viii, 4, *c.* 650 B.C.

O God! that bread should be so dear,
And flesh and blood so cheap!

>THOMAS HOOD, 1798-1845, *Song of the Shirt*

If the people have no bread let them eat cake.

>Ascribed to MARIE ANTOINETTE, 1755-1793,
>but found in ROUSSEAU's *Confessions*, 1737-1741

How is it that these silly people are so clamorous for
bread, when they can buy such nice brioches for a
few sous?

>Ascribed to the DUCHESSE DE POLIGNAC, 1749-1793

Hate of the millions who have choked you down,
In country kitchen or house in town,
With a hate more hot than the hate of the Gun—
Bread Pudding!

>BERT LESTON TAYLOR, 1866-1921

A smell like an eating-house and a pastrycook's next
door to each other, with a laundress's next door to
that. That was the pudding.

>CHARLES DICKENS, 1812-1870, *A Christmas Carol*

Honest bread is very well—it's butter that makes the
temptation.   D. W. JERROLD, 1803-1857, *The Catspaw*

Butter and honey shall he [Immanuel] eat, that he
may know to refuse the evil, and choose the good.

>*Isaiah* vii, 14

They say butter is gold in the morning, silver at noon, but it is lead at night.

JONATHAN SWIFT, 1667-1745, *Dialogue*

One cannot shoot with butter but with guns.

PAUL JOSEPH GOEBBELS, 1897-1945, Speech

Guns will make us powerful; butter will only make us fat. HERMANN GOERING, 1893-1946, Radio Speech

While ladling butter from alternate tubs
Stubbs butters Freeman, Freeman butters Stubbs.

J. F. T. ROGERS, 1823-1890

# of SOUPS & SALADS

BEAUTIFUL Soup, so rich and green,
Waiting in a hot tureen!
Who for such dainties would not stoop!
Soup of the evening, beautiful Soup!
Soup of the evening, beautiful Soup!

LEWIS CARROLL, 1832-1898

To make good soup, the pot must only simmer or
"smile."   FRENCH PROVERB

Whoever tells a lie cannot be pure in heart—and only
the pure in heart can make a good soup.

LUDWIG VAN BEETHOVEN, 1770-1827

At dinners where there are a number of guests, the vessel, containing the soup, that is to say, the tureen, does not appear at all, upon the table. It is placed on the dining-room buffet; the soup is served to the guests in soup-bowls, by servants.

At family dinners, the tureen is placed before the person doing the honors for him to serve the guests, but the first is the usual method, and for all that, preferable.

For the formal as well as the informal dinner soup should be prepared with the greatest care; for, served at the beginning of the meal, it inevitably influences opinion about the meal which it precedes: soup should always be served hot.

URBAIN DUBOIS, *École des Cuisinière*

In taking soup, it is necessary to avoid lifting too much in the spoon, or filling the mouth so full as almost to stop the breath.

ST. JOHN BAPTIST DE LA SALLE, 1651-1719,
The Rules of Christian Manners and Civility

Never blow your soup if it is too hot, but wait until it cools. Never raise your plate to your lips, but eat with your spoon.

C. B. HARTLEY, *The Gentlemen's Book of Etiquette*, 1873

Taking soup gracefully, under the difficulties opposed to it by a dinner dress at that time fashionable, was reared into an art about forty-five years ago by a

Frenchman who lectured on it to ladies in London; and the most brilliant duchess of that day, viz. the Duchess of Devonshire, was among his best pupils.

THOMAS DE QUINCEY, 1785-1859, *Conversation*

Eloise,—Perhaps you are not aware of the reason why the great majority of the people in this country [England] are opposed to, and even accused of not liking soup; the simple reason is, that every receipt described in most Cookery Books, is so complicated and expensive, that they cannot afford either the money, time, or attention to prepare it.

ALEXIS SOYER, 1809-1858, *A Shilling Cookery for the People*

"Clam or Cod?" she repeated.

"A clam for supper? a cold clam; is *that* what you mean, Mrs. Hussey?" says I; "but that's a rather cold and clammy reception in the winter time, ain't it, Mrs. Hussey?"

But being in a great hurry to resume scolding the man in the purple shirt, who was waiting for it in the entry, and seeming to hear nothing but the word "clam," Mrs. Hussey hurried toward an open door leading to the kitchen, and bawling out "clam for two," disappeared.

"Queequeg," said I, "do you think that we can make out a supper for us both on one clam?"

However, a warm savory steam from the kitchen served to belie the apparently cheerless prospect before us. But when that smoking chowder came in, the mystery was delightfully explained. Oh, sweet friends! hearken to me. It was made of small juicy clams, scarcely bigger than hazel nuts, mixed with pounded ship biscuit, and salted pork cut up into little flakes; the whole enriched with butter, and plentifully seasoned with pepper and salt. Our appetites being sharpened by the frosty voyage, and in particular, Queequeg seeing his favorite fishing food before him, and the chowder being surpassingly excellent, we despatched it with great expedition: when leaning back a moment and bethinking me of Mrs. Hussey's clam and cod announcement, I thought I would try a little experiment. Stepping to the kitchen door, I uttered the word "cod" with great emphasis, and resumed my seat. In a few moments the savory steam came forth again, but with a different flavor, and in good time a fine cod-chowder was placed before us.

We resumed business; and while plying our spoons in the bowl, thinks I to myself, I wonder now if this here has any effect on the head? What's that stultifying saying about chowder-headed people? "But look, Queequeg, ain't that a live eel in your bowl? Where's your harpoon?"

Fishiest of all fishy places was the Try Pots, which well deserved its name; for the pots there were always boiling chowders. Chowder for breakfast, and chowder for dinner, and chowder for supper, till you began to look for fish-bones coming through your clothes. The area before the house was paved with

clam-shells. Mrs. Hussey wore a polished necklace of codfish vertebrae; and Hosea Hussey had his account books bound in superior old shark-skin. There was a fish flavor to the milk too, which I could not at all account for, till one morning happening to take a stroll along the beach among some fishermen's boats, I saw Hosea's brindled cow feeding on fish remnants, and marching along the sand with each foot in a cod's decapitated head, looking very slip-shod I assure ye.
HERMAN MELVILLE,
1819-1891, *Moby Dick*

As thin as the homeopathic soup that was made by boiling the shadow of a pigeon that had starved to death.
ABRAHAM LINCOLN, 1809-1865,
Speech in Quincy, Ill.

Birds in their little nests agree
  With Chinamen, but not with me.
HILAIRE BELLOC, 1870-1953, *New Cautionary Tales*

Bouillabaise is only good because cooked by the French, who, if they cared to try, could produce an excellent and nutritious substitute out of cigar stumps and empty match boxes.
NORMAN DOUGLAS, 1868-1952, *Siren Land*

The Sallet, which of old came in last,
Why now with it begin we our Repast?
MARTIAL, 40?-?102, *Epigrammata*

But there now starts up a Question, Whether it were better, or more proper, to Begin with Sallets, or End and Conclude with them? Some think the harder Meats should first be eaten for better Concoction; others, those of easiest Digestion, to make way, and prevent Obstruction; and this makes for our Sallets, Horarii, and Fugaces Fructus (as they call 'em) to be eaten first of all, as agreeable to the general Opinion of the great Hippocrates, and Galen, and of Celsus before him. . . . But of later Times, they were constant at the Ante-coenia, eating plentifully of Sallet, especially of Lettuce, and more refrigerating Herbs. Nor without Cause: For drinking liberally they were found to expell, and allay the Fumes and Vapors of the genial Compotation, the spirituous Liquor gently conciliating Sleep: Besides, that being of a crude nature, more dispos'd, and apt to fluctuate, corrupt, and disturb a surcharg'd Stomach; and they thought convenient to begin with Sallets, and innovate the ancient Usage. . . .

The Spaniards, notwithstanding, eat but sparingly of Herbs at Dinner, especially Lettuce, beginning with Fruit, even before the Olio and Hot Meats come to the Table . . .

JOHN EVELYN, 1620-1706, *Acetaria*

What is more refreshing than salads when your appetite seems to have deserted you, or even after a capacious dinner—the nice, fresh, green, and crisp salad, full of life and health, which seems to invigorate the palate and dispose the masticating powers to a much longer duration. The herbaceous plants which exist fit for food for men, are more numerous than may be imagined, and when we reflect how many of these, for want of knowledge, are allowed to rot and decompose in the fields and gardens, we ought, without loss of time, to make ourselves acquainted with their different nature and forms, and vary our food as the season changes.

Although nature has provided different herbs and plants as food for man at various periods of the year, and perhaps at one period more abundant than another, when there are so many ready to assist in purifying and cleansing the blood, yet it would be advisable to grow some at other seasons, in order that the health may be properly nourished.

ALEXIS SOYER, 1809-1858, *A Shilling Cookery for the People*

The salad—for which, like everybody else I ever met, he had a special receipt of his own.

GEORGE DU MAURIER, 1834-1896, *Trilby*

Sallets in general consist of certain Esculent Plants and Herbs, improv'd by Culture, Industry, and Art of the Gard'ner: Or, as others say, they are a Composition of Edule Plants and Roots of several kinds, to be eaten Raw or Green, Blanch'd, or Candied; simple —*per se*, or intermingl'd with others according to the Season. The Boil'd, Bak'd, Pickl'd, or otherwise disguis'd, variously accomodated by the skilful

Cooks, to render them grateful to the more feminine Palat, or Herbs rather for the Pot, &c. challenge not the name of Sallet so properly here, tho' sometimes mention'd; And therefore,

Those who Criticize not so nicely upon the Word, seem to distinguish the Olera (which were never eaten Raw) from Aceteria, which were never Boil'd.

A great deal more of this Learned Stuff were to be pick'd up from the Cumini Sectores, and impertinently Curious; whilst as it concerns the business in hand, we are by Sallet to understand a particular Composition of certain Crude and fresh Herbs, such as usually are, or may be safely eaten with some Acetous Juice, Oyl, Salt, &c. to give them a grateful Gust and Vehicle . . . But of this enough, and perhaps too much; least whilst I write of Salt and Sallet, I appear my self Insipid... JOHN EVELYN, 1620-1706, *Acetaria*

Take endive . . . like love it is bitter;
　Take beet . . . like love it is red;
Crisp leaf of lettuce shall glitter,
　And cress from the rivulet's bed;
Anchovies foam-born, like the Lady
　Whose beauty has maddened this bard;
And olives from groves that are shady;
　And eggs—boil'em hard.
　　　　MORTIMER COLLINS, 1827-1876, parodying Swinburne

In a good salad there should be more oil than vinegar or salt.　　Ascribed to ST. FRANCIS DE SALES, 1567-1622

According to the Spanish proverb, four persons are wanted to make a good salad: a spendthrift for oil, a miser for vinegar, a counsellor for salt, and a madman to stir all up.

ABRAHAM HAYWARD, 1801-1884, *The Art of Dining*

Oh, herbaceous treat!
'Twould tempt the dying anchorite to eat;
Back to the world he'd turn his fleeting soul,
And plunge his fingers in the salad bowl;
Serenely full the epicure would say,
"Fate cannot harm me,—I have dined today."

SYDNEY SMITH, 1771-1845,
A Receipt for a Salad

He that sups upon salad, goes not to bed fasting.

THOMAS FULLER, 1608-1661, *Gnomologia*

Let first the onion flourish there,
Rose among the roots, the maiden-fair
Wine-scented and poetic soul
Of the capacious salad bowl.

ROBERT LOUIS STEVENSON, 1850-1894, *To a Gardener*

The better the salad the worse the dinner.

ITALIAN PROVERB

A sallet without wine is raw, unwholesome, dangerous.

RANDLE COTGRAVE, d. 1634?, *French-English Dictionary*

For if on Wine you Lettuce eat,
It floats upon the stomach—   HORACE, 65-8 B.C., *Satires*

Lettuce cooleth the heat of the stomacke, called the
heart-burning; and helpeth it when it is troubled
with choler: it quenches thirst and causeth sleepe.
    Lettuce maketh a pleasant sallad, being eaten raw
with vinegar, oile, and a little salt: but if it be
boiled it is sooner digested, and nourisheth more.
                               JOHN GERARD, 1545-1612, *Herball*

Lettuce: It is of all herbs, the best and wholesomest
for the hot seasons, for young men, and them that
abound with choler, and also for the sanguine, and
such as have hot stomachs.
           TOBIAS VENNER, 1577-1660, *Via Recta ad vitam longam*

Lettuce is like conversation: it must be fresh and
crisp, and so sparkling that you scarcely notice the
bitter in it.
           C. D. WARNER, 1829-1900, *My Summer in a Garden*

It is said that the effect of eating too much lettuce
is "soporific."
        BEATRIX POTTER, 1866-1943, *The Tale of the Flopsie Bunnies*

A cucumber should be well sliced, and dressed with
pepper and vinegar, and then thrown out as good
for nothing.
        SAMUEL JOHNSON, 1709-1784, Boswell's *Tour to the Hebrides*

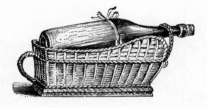

o𝒻 WINE & BEER

𝓑ACCHUS, that first from out the purple grape
Crush'd the sweet poison of misus'd wine.
JOHN MILTON, 1608-1674, Comus

Wine is the most healthful and most hygienic of
beverages. LOUIS PASTEUR, 1822-1895

Every man at the beginning doth set forth good
wine; and when men have well drunk, then that
which is worse. John, ii, 10, c. 115

Attic honey thickens the nectar-like Falernian.
Such drink deserves to be mixed by Ganymede.
MARTIAL, c. 40-c. 102, Epigrammata

It's a Naive Domestic Burgundy without any Breeding, But I Think You'll be Amused by its Presumption.   JAMES THURBER, 1894-1961,
Title of cartoon in the *New Yorker*

I like best the wine drunk at the cost of others.
     DIOGENES, the Cynic, 412?-323 B.C.

"I rather like bad wine," said Mr. Mountchesney: "one gets so bored with good wine."
     BENJAMIN DISRAELI, 1804-1881, *Sybil*

When men drink wine they are rich, they are busy, they push lawsuits, they are happy, they help their friends.   ARISTOPHANES, 448?-380? B.C., *The Knights*

One barrel of wine can work more miracles than a church full of saints.   ITALIAN PROVERB

Wine makes old wives wenches.
     JOHN CLARKE, *Paroemiologia Anglo-Latina*, 1639

Drink no longer water, but use a little wine for thy stomach's sake and thine other infirmities.
     I *Timothy* v, 23, *c.* 60

There is not a corner nor burrow in all my body where this wine does not ferret out my thirst.
     FRANCOIS RABELAIS,
c. 1494-*c.* 1533, *Gargantua* I

He is believed to have liked port, but to have said of claret that "it would be port if it could."

RICHARD BENTLEY, 1662-1742

She believed he had been drinking too much of Mr. Weston's good wine.   JANE AUSTEN,
1775-1817, *Emma*

If you say, "Would there were no wine" because of the drunkards, then you must say going on by degrees, "Would there were no steel," because of the murderers, "Would there were no night," because of the thieves, "Would there were no light," because of the informers, and "Would there were no women," because of adultery.

ST. JOHN CHRYSOSTOM, *Homilies* I, c. 388

Wine does not intoxicate men: men intoxicate themselves.   CHINESE PROVERB

When wine is in the wit is out.

THOMAS FULLER, 1608-1661, *Gnomologia*

Wine gives a man nothing. It neither gives him knowledge nor wit; it only animates a man, and enables him to bring out what a dread of the company has repressed. This is one of the disadvantages of wine: it makes a man mistake words for thoughts.

SAMUEL JOHNSON,
1709-1784, Boswell's *Life*

Take counsel in wine, but resolve afterwards in water.
BENJAMIN FRANKLIN, 1706-1790,
Poor Richard's Almanack

Wine is a mocker, strong drink is raging: and who-
soever is deceived thereby is not wise.
Proverbs xx, 1, *c.* 350 B.C.

Howl, all ye drinkers of wine.
Joel i, 5, *c.* 350 B.C.

Finding my head goes weak nowadays, if I come to
drink wine, and therefore hope that I shall leave it
off of myself which I pray God I could do.
SAMUEL PEPYS, 1633-1703, *Diary*

There is a crying for wine in the streets; all joy is
darkened, the mirth of the land is gone.
Isaiah, xxiv, 11, *c.* 700 B.C.

No government could survive without champagne.
Champagne in the throat of our diplomatic people
is like oil in the wheels of an engine.
JOSEPH DARGENT, in *New York Herald Tribune*, July 21, 1955

The sign of a ceremonial dinner. Pretend to despise
it, saying: "It's really not a wine." Arouses the en-
thusiasm of petty folk. Russia drinks more of it than
France. Has been the medium for spreading French
ideas throughout Europe. During the Regency people

did nothing but drink champagne. But technically
one doesn't drink it, one samples it.
GUSTAVE FLAUBERT, 1821-1880, *Dictionnaire des Idées Reçu*

"To some swell Night Club we must roam,"
    Said he, "and drink champagne."
But she said: "We can stay at home,
    And still be raising Cain."
THOMAS A. DALY, 1871-1948, *The First New Year's Eve*

Here's to champagne, the drink divine
That makes us forget our troubles:
It's made of a dollar's worth of wine
And three dollars worth of bubbles.   ANONYMOUS

The quality of the champagne may be judged by the
amount of noise the cork makes when it is popped.
H. L. MENCKEN, 1880-1956 &
GEORGE JEAN NATHAN, 1882-1958, *The American Credo*

Champagne certainly gives one werry gentlemanly
ideas, but for a continuance, I don't know but what
I should prefer mild ale.
R. S. SURTEES, 1803-1864, *Jorrock's Jaunts and Jollities*

Lo! the poor toper whose untutored sense,
Sees bliss in ale, and can with wine dispense;
Whose head proud fancy never taught to steer,
Beyond the muddy ecstasies of beer.
GEORGE CRABBE, 1754-1832, *Inebriety*

If smirking wine be wanting here,
There's that which drowns all care, stout beer.
                    ROBERT HERRICK, 1591-1674, *Hesperides*

Beer is chiefly to be desired in the Summer, and it is
a drink (believe me) for all constitutions, but especially for the cholerick and melancholick most
wholesome.
            TOBIAS VENNER, 1577-1660, *Via recta ad vitam longam*

I wish to see this beverage become common instead
of the whisky which kills one-third of our citizens
and ruins their families.
            THOMAS JEFFERSON, 1743-1826, Letter to Charles Yancey

They had beer to drink, very strong when not mixed
with water, but agreeable to those accustomed to it.
                    XENOPHON, 434?-?355 B.C., *Anabasis*

Beer makes the hero.   CZECH PROVERB

When beer goes in wit comes out.   DANISH PROVERB

Beer and bread make the cheeks red.   GERMAN PROVERB

O Beer! O Hodgson, Guinness, Alsoop, Bass
Names that should be on every tongue.
                    C. S. CALVERLEY, 1831-1884, *Ballad*

Do not drink beer if you want to avoid colds.
            GUSTAVE FLAUBERT, 1821-1880, *Dictionnaire des Idées Reçu*

Life is with such all beer and skittles;
They are not difficult to please
About their victuals.
C. S. CALVERLY, 1831-1884, *Contentment*

What two ideas are more inseparable than Beer and
Britannia?   SYDNEY SMITH, 1771-1845

Ale: The liquor is the Englishman's ancientist and
wholesomest drink, and servest many for meat and
cloth too.   THOMAS CAREW, 1595-1639

Then to the spicy nut brown ale.
JOHN MILTON, 1608-1674, *L'Allegro*

I have fed purely upon ale; I have eat my ale, drank
my ale, and I always sleep upon ale.
GEORGE FARQUHAR, 1678-1707, *The Beaux' Stratagem*

Mine host was full of ale and history.
R. CORBET, 1620-1680

". . . he came in here, . . . ordered a glass of this ale—
would order it—I told him not—drank it and fell
dead. It was too ald for him. It oughtn't to be
drawn; that's a fact."
CHARLES DICKENS, 1812-1870, *David Copperfield*

And a few men talked of freedom, while England
talked of ale.   G. K. CHESTERTON, 1874-1936, *The Secret People*

o*f* SAUCES
& SEASONINGS

QRT is not a special sauce applied to ordinary cooking; it is the cooking itself if it is good.

> w. r. lethaby, *Form in Civilization*

I would eat my own father with such a sauce.

> grimod de la reyniere, *L'Almanach des Gourmands*, 1803

Though the sauce be good, yet you need not forsake the meat for it. thomas fuller, 1608-1661, *Gnomologia*

It is the sauce that makes the fish edible.

> FRENCH PROVERB

There are in England sixty different religious sects, but only one sauce.   F. CARACCIOLI, 1752-1799

What's sauce for the goose is sauce for the gander.
ENGLISH PROVERB

Appetite is the best sauce.   FRENCH PROVERB

The best sauce in the world is hunger.
CERVANTES, 1547-1616, *Don Quixote*

Anise: An aromatic plant of the family of Umbelliferae, abundant all over Europe, Egypt, and Syria, but especially in Italy and above all in Rome, where it is the despair of the foreigners who cannot escape its flavor or its aroma. They put it into their cakes and break. The Neapolitans put it into everything. . . . In Germany it is the principal condiment in the bread served everywhere with an accompaniment of figs and diced pears. This is called pumpernickel. The name is derived from the exclamation of a horseman who, after tasting it, gave the rest to his horse, whose name was Nick, saying "Bon pour Nick!" which, with the German accent became *Pompernick*.
ALEXANDRE DUMAS, 1802-1870

Eating cress makes one witty.   GREEK PROVERB

He who hath money and capers, is provided for Lent.
THOMAS FULLER, 1654-1734, *Gnomologia*

Fenell is of great use to trim up and strowe upon
fish, as also to boyle or put among fish of divers
sorts, Cowcumbers pickled and other fruits, etc. the
rootes are used with Parsley rootes to be boyled in
broths. The seed is much used to put in Pippin pies
and divers others such baked fruits, as also into
bread, to give it the better relish. The Sweet Cardus
Fenell being sent by Sir Henry Wotton to John
Tradescante had likewise a large direction with it
how to dress it, for they used to white it after it hath
been transplanted for their uses, which by reason of
sweetnesse by nature, and the tendernesse by art,
causeth it to be more delightfull to the taste.

JOHN PARKINSON, 1567-1650, *Paradisus Terrestris*

Fennel: A decoction of the leaves and root is good
for serpent bites, and to neutralize vegetable poison,
as mushrooms, etc.					NICHOLAS CULPEPPER, 1616-1654,
The New English Physician Enlarged

The pouder of the seed of Fennell drunke for certaine
daies together fasting preserveth the eyesight: whereof was written this Distichon following:
    Of Fennell, Roses, Vervain, Rue, and Celandine,
    Is made a water good to clere the sight of eine.
JOHN GERARD, 1545-1612, *Herball*

Let me see; what am I to buy for our sheep-shearing
feast? "Three pounds of sugar; five pounds of cur-
rants; rice," what will this sister of mine do with

rice? . . . I must have saffron, to color the warden
pies; mace, dates,—none; that's out of my note; nut-
megs seven; a race or two of ginger,—but that I may
beg,—four pounds of prunes, and as many of raisins
o' the sun.

WILLIAM SHAKESPEARE, 1564-1616, *The Winter's Tale*

Our apothecary's shop is our garden full of potherbs,
and our doctor is a clove of garlic.

ANONYMOUS, *A Deep Snow*, 1615

Garlic is as good as ten mothers.   TELUGU PROVERB

And scorne not Garlicke like to some that thinke
It onely makes men winke, and drinke, and stinke.

ENGLISH PROVERB

If one does not eat garlic one does not stink.

HEBREW PROVERB

Of herbs, and other country messes
Which the neat-handed Phyllis dresses.

JOHN MILTON, 1608-1674, *L'Allegro*

Let an ascetic eat no honey, no flesh, no mushrooms,
nor any thing grown on plowed ground.

The Code of MANU VI, *c.* 100

Mayonnaise: One of the sauces which serve the
French in place of a state religion.

AMBROSE BIERCE, 1842-1914?, *The Devil's Dictionary*

Mushroom: Divers esteeme those for the best which grow in medowes, and upon mountaines and hilly places, as Horace saith,

The medow Mushroms are in kinde the beste;
It is ill trusting any of the rest.

Galen affirmes, that they are all very cold and moist, and therefore to approach unto a venomous and murtherous facultie, and ingender a clammy, pituitous, and cold nutriment if they be eaten. To conclude, few of them are good to be eaten, and most of them do suffocate and strangle the eater. Therefore I give my advice unto those that love such strange and new fangled meates, to beware of licking honey among thornes, least the sweetnesse of the one do not countervaile the sharpnesse and pricking of the other.   JOHN GERARD, 1545-1612, *Herball*

Mustard: Good only in Dijon. Ruins the stomach.
          GUSTAVE FLAUBERT, 1821-1880, *Dictionnaire des Idées Reçu*

After meat, mustard.
When there's no more use of it.   JOHN RAY, 1627-1705

Peper, *Piper*; hot and dry in a high degree; of approv'd Vertue against all flatulency proceeding from cold and phlegmatic Constitutions, and generally all Crudities whatsoever; and therefore for being of universal use to correct and temper the cooler Herbs, and such as abound in moisture; It is a never to be omitted ingredient of our *Sallets*; provided it be not too minutely beaten (as we oft find it) to an almost impalpable Dust, which is very pernicious and frequently adheres and sticks in the folds of the Stomach, where, instead of promoting Concoction, it often causes a *Cardialgium*, and fires the Blood: It should therefore be grosly contus'd only.

JOHN EVELYN, 1620-1706, *Acetaria*

There are six flavors, and of them all salt is the chief.

SANSCRIT PROVERB

Salt is the policeman of taste: it keeps the various flavors of a dish in order and restrains the stronger from tyrannizing over the weaker. MALCOLM DE CHAZAL

Salt is what makes things taste bad when it isn't in them. ANONYMOUS

Salt is white and pure—there is something holy in salt. NATHANIEL HAWTHORNE,
1804-1864, *American Note-Books*

Do not salt other people's food. BULGARIAN PROVERB

Before you make a friend eat a bushel of salt with him. GEORGE HERBERT, 1593-1633, *Outlandish Proverbs*

I was at first at a great loss for Salt; but Custom soon reconciled the Want of it; and I am confident that the frequent use of Salt among us is an Effect of

Luxury, and was first introduced as a provocative to Drink; except where it necessary for preserving of flesh in long Voyages, or in Places remote from great Markets. For we observe no animal to be fond of it but Man. And as to myself, when I left this Country, it was a great while before I could endure the taste of it in anything that I eat.

JONATHAN SWIFT, 1667-1745, *Gulliver's Travels*

If you beat it, spice will smell the sweeter.

THOMAS FULLER, 1608-1661, *Gnomologia*

The truffle is not an outright aphrodisiac, but it may, in certain circumstances make women more affectionate and men more amiable.

BRILLAT-SAVARIN, 1755-1826, *Physiologie du Goût*

You gotta have a swine to show you where the truffles are.

EDWARD ALBEE, 1928-   , *Who's Afraid of Virginia Woolf?*

You first parent of the human race . . . who ruined yourself for an apple, what might you have done for a truffled turkey?

BRILLAT-SAVARIN, 1755-1826, *Physiologie du Goût*

The sweetest wine turneth to the sharpest vinegar.

JOHN LYLY, 1554?-1606, *Euphues*

Vinegar, the son of wine.   HEBREW PROVERB

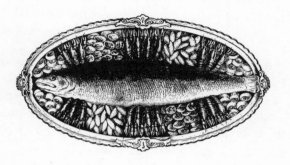

# of FISH & FOWL

THESE shall ye eat of all that are in the waters: whatsoever hath fins and scales in the waters, in the seas, and in the rivers, them shall ye eat.

Leviticus xi, 9

We remember the fish, which we did eat in Egypt freely; the cucumbers, the melons, and the leeks, and the onions, and the garlic.   *Numbers* xi, 5, *c.* 700 B.C.

Fish dinners will make a man spring like a flea.

THOMAS JORDAN, 1612-1685

Only eat fresh fish and ripened rice.   CHINESE PROVERB

Give a man a fish, and you feed him for a day,
Teach him to fish, and you feed him for a lifetime.

CHINESE PROVERB

Little fish are sweet.   DUTCH PROVERB

Nor is it enough to sweep up fish from the expensive
stall, not knowing which are better with sauce, and
which, if broiled, will tempt the tired guest to raise
himself once more upon his elbow.

HORACE, 65-8 B.C., Satires

With the audacity of true culinary genius, fried fish
is always served cold.

ISRAEL ZANGWILL, 1864-1926, Children of the Ghetto

Fish must swim thrice—once in water, a second time
in the sauce, and third time in wine in the stomach.

JOHN RAY, 1627-1705, English Proverbs

Very well. But what sense tells you whether this
pike gasping here was caught in the Tiber or in the
sea, whether in the eddies between the bridges or
just at the mouth of the Tuscan river? You foolish
fellow, you praise a three-pound mullet, which you
must needs cut up into single portions. 'Tis the look,
I see, that takes you. Why then detest a very long
pike? It is, of course, because nature has made the
pike large, and the mullet light of weight. Only a
stomach that seldom feels hunger scorns things
common.   HORACE, 65-8 B.C., Satires

Across the bridge began the vegetable and fruit market, where whole Hollands of cabbage and Spains of
onions opened on the view, with every other succulent and toothsome growth; and beyond this we
entered the glory of Rialto, the fish-market, which
is now more lavishly supplied than at any other season. It was picturesque and full of gorgeous color;
for the fish of Venice seem all to catch the rainbow
hues of the lagoon. There is a certain kind of red
mullet, called *triglia*, which is as rich and tender in
its dyes as if it had never swam in waters less glorious
than that which crimsons under October sunsets.
But a fish-market, even at Rialto, with fishermen in
scarlet caps and *triglie* in sunset splendors, is only a
fish-market after all: it is wet and slimy under foot,
and the innumerable gigantic eels, writhing everywhere, set the soul asquirm, and soon-sated curiosity slides willingly away.

WILLIAM DEAN HOWELLS, 1837-1920, *Venetian Life*

Though a man eats fish till his guts crack, yet if he
eat no flesh he fasts. JOHN TAYLOR, 1580-1653, *Jack-a-Lent*

What an idiot is man to believe that abstaining from
flesh, and eating fish, which is so much more delicate
and delicious, constitutes fasting.

NAPOLEON I, 1769-1821, To Barry E. O'Mara

A man may eat fish with the worm that hath eat of a
king, and eat of the fish that hath fed of that worm.

WILLIAM SHAKESPEARE, 1564-1616, *Hamlet*

This piece of cod passes all understanding.

SIR EDWIN LUTYENS, 1869-1944,
Attributed remark in restaurant

Bream: . . . But he can still be served up as an excellent stew, provided always that he is full-grown, and has swum all his life in clear running water.

THOMAS LOVE PEACOCK, 1785-1866, *Gryll Grange*

. . . He did odd jobs on the fish docks, and he fed us fish until the bones stuck out of our ears. Comb my hair in the morning, I'd comb out a handful of bones. It got so my stomach rose and fell with the tide. Fish, fish! I was almost grown before I found out people ate anything else.   CHARLES CASSELL

in J. Mitchell's *McSorley's Wonderful Saloon*, 1943

A crabbe, breke hym a-sonder in a dysshe, make ye shelle cleane and put him in the stuffe againe; tempre it with vynegre and pouder, then cover it with brede, and send it to the kytchyn to hete; then set it to your soverayne, and breke the grete clawes, and laye them in a disshe.

WYNKYN DE WORDE, d. ?1534, *Boke of Kervynge*

The Crab is not easily digested; it is a meate best agreeing with those that are of a cholericke temperature, and that have hot stomacks.

TOBIAS VENNER, 1577-1660,
Via recta ad vitam longam

Among all fishes that are pleasant in taste and not wholesome, the Yeele are most in use, which, as they be engendered of the very earth, dirt and mire, without generation or Spawne, they be of a slimie substance, clammie and greatly stopping, whereby they are noysome to the voice.

HENRY COGAN, fl. 1650, *Haven of Health*

Of all the fish in the sea herring is king.

JAMES HOWELL, 1594?-1666, *Proverbs*

A land with lots of herring can get along with few doctors.   DUTCH PROVERB

And like a lobster boil'd, the morn
From black to red began to turn.

SAMUEL BUTLER, 1612-1680, *Hudibras*

Octopus: This frightfully hideous mollusc is nevertheless eaten, especially in Naples. It is boiled and served with tomato sauce, or, more often, it is boiled and then fried. We ate one, called a *calmaro* in Italy, and discovered that it has a remarkable resemblance to fried calf's ear.   ALEXANDRE DUMAS, 1802-1870

Practically all the littleneck and cherrystone clams served on the half shell in New York restaurants come out of the black mud of Long Island bays. They are the saltiest, cleanest, and biggest-bellied clams in the world. . . .

He gave me one and we squatted on the deck and went to work opening the cherries. When the valves were pried apart, the rich clam liquor dribbled out. The flesh of the cherries was a delicate pink. On the cups of some of the shells were splotches of deep purple; Indians used to hack such splotches out of clamshells for wampum. Fresh from the coal-black mud and uncontaminated by ketchup or sauce, they were the best clams I have ever eaten. The mate sat on the hatch and watched us.

"Aren't you going to have any?" I asked.

"I wouldn't put one of those damned things in my mouth if I was perishing to death," he said, "I'm working on this buoy-boat for ten years and I'm yet to eat a clam."

JOSEPH MITCHELL, *McSorley's Wonderful Saloon*, 1943

Oysters are amatory food.

LORD BYRON, 1788-1824, *Don Juan*

Our oisters are generallie forborne in the foure hot moneths of the yeare, that is Maie, June, Julie, and August, which are void of the letter R.

WILLIAM HARRISON, 1534-1593,
Description of England

Oysters are more beautiful than any religion. . . . There's nothing in Christianity or Buddhism that quite matches the sympathetic unselfishness of an oyster.   SAKI, 1870-1916, *Chronicles of Clovis*

A loaf of bread, the Walrus said
　Is what we chiefly need:
Pepper and vinegar besides
　Are very good indeed—
Now if you're ready, Oysters, dear,
　We can begin to feed!
LEWIS CARROLL, 1832-1898, Through the Looking-Glass

Oysters: Few among those who go to restaurants
realize that the man who first opened one must have
been a man of genius and a profound observer.
BRILLAT-SAVARIN, 1755-1826, Physiologie du Goût

King James was wont to say, "He was a very valiant
man who first ventured on eating of oysters."
THOMAS FULLER, 1608-1661, Worthies of England

He was a bold man that first ate an oyster.
ENGLISH PROVERB

It is more useful, perhaps, to know my host at the
Blue Boar in Picadilly died of eating too many
oysters, than how Marshall Turenne was killed in
the trenches.
ELIZABETH MONTAGU, 1720-1800, to Lord Lyttelton

Let's sing a song of glory to Themistocles O'Shea,
Who ate a dozen oysters on the second day of May.
STODDARD KING, 1889-1933,
The Man Who Dared

He [Bismarck] also confesses a weakness for fried oysters; this, in my opinion, is treason to gastronomy.

JULES HOCHE, *Bismarck at Home*, 1888

Lady S. They say oysters are a cruel meat, because we eat them alive; then they are an uncharitable meat for we leave nothing to the poor; and they are an ungodly meat because we never say grace.

JONATHAN SWIFT, 1667-1745, *Dialogues*

As for oysters to which the Parisians are so partial, a great difference is made between those which arrive by boat and those which come by stage. These last which are distributed in baskets from the place of their unloading, from time immemorial in the Rue Montorgueil, are always fresher and more delicate.

The usual way oysters are eaten is raw before the soup. Many people doubt that they can be served any other way and, at the most, permit them to be seasoned with a pinch of pepper and the juice of a slice of lemon. What would they say when they learn that there are more than twenty ways of dressing them? . . .

They are, as we have already noted, the usual, and in some ways, obligatory, preface to a winter lunch. But it is a preface which often happens to come very expensive, because of the guests lack of discretion, who swallow them into their stomachs by the hundreds because of their silly vain, self-love. An enjoyment doubly insipid, in that they bring no real pleasure and often distress a worthy Amphitrion. It is proven by experience that, above five or six dozen, oysters certainly cease to be a pleasure.

GRIMOD DE LA REYNIERE,
Almanach des Gourmands, 1803

Oysters: Nobody eats them any more; too expensive.

GUSTAVE FLAUBERT, 1821-1880,
Dictionnaire des Idées Reçu

Once taste porpoise, and all other foods will be insipid.   CHINESE PROVERB

Porpoises are indeed to this day considered fine eating. The meat is made into balls about the size of billiard balls, and being well seasoned and spiced might be taken for turtle-balls or veal balls. The old monks of Dumferline were very fond of them. They had a great porpoise grant from the crown.

HERMAN MELVILLE, 1819-1891, *Moby Dick*

The common or harbour Porpoise of the North Atlantic and Pacific was once considered a delicacy in this country, as are other Cetaceans in other lands at the present day. It formed a royal dish even so recently as the time of Henry VIII. The sauce recommended by Dr. Caius for the "fish" was made of crumbs of fine bread, vinegar and sugar. Considered to be a fish, it was allowed to be eaten on fast days.

FRANK E. BEDDARD, *A Book of Whales*, 1900

The British bar-shrimp was brought upon its finger
of damp toast, from its circular glassware.

PERCY WYNDAM LEWIS, 1886-1957, *The Apes of God*

Sing a song of sixpence,
A pocket full of rye;
Four and twenty blackbirds,
Baked in a pie.

When the pie was opened,
The birds began to sing;
Wasn't that a dainty dish,
To set before the king?

NURSERY RHYME

I want there to be no peasant in my kingdom so poor
that he is unable to have a chicken in his pot on
Sundays.   HENRI IV OF FRANCE, 1553-1610

The capon is above all other foules praised, for as
much as it is easily digested.

SIR THOMAS ELYOT, *c.* 1490-1546, *Castel of Helth*

As long as I have fat turtle doves, a fig for your lettuce, my friend, and you may keep your shell-fish
to yourself. I have no desire to waste my appetite.

MARTIAL, *c.* A.D. 39-104, *Epigrammata*

I quoted his own beautiful address to the stock dove.
He said, once in a wood Mrs. Wordsworth and a lady

were walking, when the stock dove was cooing. A
farmer's wife coming by said to herself, "Oh, I do
like stock doves!" Mrs. Wordsworth, in all her en-
thusiasm for Wordsworth's poetry, took the old
woman to her heart; "but," continued the old woman, "some like them in a pie; for my part there's
nothing like them stewed in onions."

BENJAMIN ROBERT HAYDON,
1786-1846, *Autobiography*

Serve a duck whole, but eat only the breast and neck;
the rest send back to the cook.

MARTIAL, *c.* A.D. 39-104, *Epigrammata*

Our people esteem the goose chiefly on account of the
excellence of the liver, which attains a very large
size when the bird is crammed. When the liver is
thoroughly soaked in honey and milk, it becomes
specially large. It is a moot question who first made
such an excellent discovery—whether it was Scipio
Martellus, a man of consular rank, or Marcus
Sestius, a Roman knight. However, there is no doubt
that it was Messalinus Cotia who first cooked the
web feet of geese and served them up with cock's
combs, for I must award the palm of the kitchen to
the man who is deserving of it. This bird, wonderful
to relate, comes all the way from the Morini to
Rome on its own feet: the weary geese are placed in
front, and those following by a natural pressure urge
them on.   PLINY, the elder, A.D. 23-79

The goose has long been domesticated, figures of two species figuring on many Egyptian monuments, the Egyptian Goose, *anser egyptiacos*, and the Gray Goose, *anser ferus*, the latter being the bird which, by its vigilance, saved the Roman capital from the Gauls. From the Gray Goose all our domestic breeds have descended.

E. G. BOULENGER, *A Naturalist at the Dinner Table*, 1927

Larks are not fit for the spit that do not weigh over 13 oz. to the doz.

DR. LISTER, 1665-1714, Queen Anne's physician

Yet, if a peacock be served, I shall hardly root out your longing to tickle your palate with it rather than with a pullet. You are led astray by the vain appearance, because the rare bird costs gold and makes a brave show with the picture of its outspread tail—as though that had ought to do with the case! Do you eat the feathers you so admire? Does the bird look as fine when cooked? Yet, though in their meat they are on a par, to think that you crave the one rather than the other, duped by the difference in appearance!   HORACE, 65-8 B.C., *Satires*

Among the delicacies of this splendid table one sees the peacock, that noble bird, the food of lovers, and the meat of lords. Few dishes were in higher fashion in the thirteenth century, and there was scarce any noble or royal feast without it. They stuffed it with spices and sweet herbs, and covered the head with a cloth, which was constantly wetted to preserve the crown. They roasted it and served it up whole, covered after dressing with the skin and feathers on, the comb entire, and the tail spread. Some persons covered it with leaf gold, instead of its feathers, and put a piece of cotton, dipped in spirits, into its beak, to which they set fire as they put it on the table. The honour of serving it up was reserved for the ladies most distinguished for birth, rank, or beauty, one of whom, followed by the others, and attended by music, brought it up in the gold or silver dish, and set it before the master of the house, or the guest most distinguished for his courtesy and valour; or after a tournament, before the victorious knight, who was to display his skill in carving the favourite fowl, and take an oath of enterprise and valour on its head. The *Romance of Lancelot*, adopting the manner of the age in which it was written, represents King Arthur doing this office to the satisfaction of five hundred guests.

THE REV. RICHARD WAGNER, *Antiquates Culinariae*, 1791

If there is a pure and elevated pleasure in this world, it is that of roast pheasant and bread sauce;—barn-door fowls for dissenters, but for the real churchmen, the thirty-nine times articled clerk—the pheasant, the pheasant!   SYDNEY SMITH, 1771-1845

Plover is of some reputed a dainty meat, and very

wholesome; but they who so judge are much deceived; for it is of slow digestion, increaseth melancholy, and yieldeth little good nourishment for the
body.   TOBIAS VENNER, 1577-1660, *Via recta ad vitam longam*

The Tourte of Sparrows is served like that of young
pidgeons with a wine sauce.
                    FRANCOIS DE LA VARENNE, *French Cook*, 1654

You shall see in the country, in harvest time, pigeons,
though they destroy never so much corn, the farmer
dare not present his fowling-piece to them; why?
because they belong to The Lord of the Manor;
whilst your poor sparrows, belong to The Lord of
the Manor, they go to the pot for it.
                    JOHN WEBSTER, *c.* 1580-*c.* 1625, *The White Devil*

No true gastronome would countenance the killing
of a Thrush for food, even if ready to admit that it
was quite as good as a Lark, on occasions when a
Thrush found its way by accident into the classical
Steak-kidney-oyster-and-lark Pie. On the Continent,
Thrushes are killed and eaten without any qualms of
conscience, like many other small songsters, but it
is rather unexpected to find a recipe given by gentle
Mrs. Beeton for roasting one.
                    A Concise Encyclopaedia of Gastronomy, 1944

Turkeys do not come from Turkey, but from North
America, and were brought to Spain from Mexico.
                    BREWER's *Dictionary of Phrase and Fable*, 1970

In very cold weather the Turkey must be brought
into the kitchen the night before it is roasted, for
"many a Christmas dinner has been spoiled by the
Turkey having been hung up in a cold larder, and
becoming thoroughly frozen; Jack Frost has ruined
the reputation of many a Turkey Roaster."

THOMAS LOVE PEACOCK, 1785-1866,
as quoted by the editors of his *Works*

About 1524 it happened that divers things were
newly brought into England, whereupon this Rhyme
was made:

Turkeys, Carps, Hoppes, Piccarell, and Beer,
Came into England all in one year.

SIR RICHARD BAKER, 1568-1645, *Chronicles of the Kings of England*

This fowl is St. Martin's bird as the ox is St. Luke's;
and who would dare to sacrifice anything else on
this day: its roasting is obligatory on November 11:
every one, from cooks to academicians, struggles to
have a turkey and the contest raises their price, they
are then dearer than the golden pheasant. . . .

Whoever loves a turkey (and who, in this world,
doesn't) cannot hate the Jesuits, for it is to these
good fathers (who are, for all that, not geese) that
it is said that we owe the introduction of this bird
to France, where it did not tarry to acclimate to the
point where it is now native. Some claim that India
was its original home, others Numidia, but what
does it matter where it came from, provided it is ten-

der. It was in 1570 at the wedding of Charles IX
that they made their first appearance here and the
welcome they received insured their increase. The
art of raising and fattening them soon became one of
the rare and useful arts of the world. . . . Once they
survived the perils of infancy, they prospered and
their extreme gluttony made them easy to fatten
and aggravated the esteem in which they were held.
They made themselves extremely accommodating to
the desires of man and acquired in a few months the
plump breasts required of them by their protectors.

After verifying that they are young and tender,
the first care is to be assured that their flesh is not
bitter. The secret of this is not easy to communicate
delicately but as it is very good to know one will
pardon its inconvenience because of its usefulness.
The ladies, then, will not be shocked if we divulge
that it consists in inserting the index finger in the
bird's anus and then sucking the finger with a strong
intake of breath. This method is infallible. . . .

Such, in all its glory, is a young hen turkey ready
for the spit. It is, in our view, the finest of the
winged roasts, if it is not the finest it is the most
suitable for large gatherings, and it is not just on
St. Martin's Day that one should see lively guests
respectfully assembled around the opulent turkey.

GRIMOD DE LA REYNIERE, *Almanach des Gourmands*, 1803

In the olden days, when big flocks were "walked"
into London—a journey often taking a week or more

—the birds [turkeys] were protected from "cold feet" by being shod, their feet being tied up in sacking and provided with leather boots. Geese do not allow themselves to be shod, and the feet of these birds, when similarly driven, were protected by a coat of tar covered with grit. As a result the phrase to "shoe a goose" was once a cant simile for attempting a hopeless task.

E. G. BOULENGER, *A Naturalist at the Dinner Table*, 1927

If the partridge had the woodcock's thigh
It would be the best bird that ever did fly.

JOHN RAY, 1627-1705, *English Proverbs*

Some Epicures like the bird very much underdone, and direct that—a Woodcock should just be intro- duced to the Cook, for her to shew it to the fire, and then send it up to Table.

THOMAS LOVE PEACOCK, 1785-1866,

# of MEATS

In number of dishes and change of meat the nobility of England (whose cooks are for the most part musical-headed Frenchmen & strangers) do most exceed, sith there is no day in manner that passeth over their heads wherein they have not only beef, mutton, veal, lamb, kid, pork, cony, capon, pig, or so many of these as the season yieldeth, but also some portion of the red or fallow deer, beside great variety of fish and wild fowl, and thereto other delicates wherein the sweet hand of the sea-faring Portingal is not wanting; so that for a man to dine with one of them,

and to taste of every dish that standeth before him
(which few use to do, but each one feedeth upon
that meat him best liketh for the time, the beginning
of every dish notwithstanding being reserved unto
the greatest personage that sitteth at the table, to
whom it is drawn up still by the waiters as order
requireth, and from whom it descendeth again even
to the lower end, whereby each one may taste thereof), is rather to yield unto a conspiracy with a great
deal of meat for the speedy suppression of natural
health, than the use of a necessary meat to satisfy
himself with a competent repast to sustain his body
withal. WILLIAM HARRISON, 1534-1593, *Description of England*

The nearer the bone the sweeter the meat.

ENGLISH PROVERB

If you buy meat cheap, you will smell what you have
saved when it boils. ARAB PROVERB

Old meat makes good soap. ITALIAN PROVERB

Strong meat belongeth to them that are full of age.
Hebrews v, 14, *c.* 65

Much meat, much malady.

THOMAS FULLER, 1608-1661, *Gnomologia*

It is only by softening and disguising dead flesh by
culinary preparation that it is rendered susceptible

of mastication or digestion; and that the sight of its
bloody juices and raw horror does not excite in-
tolerable loathing and disgust.

PERCY BYSSHE SHELLEY, 1792-1822, *Queen Mab*, Notes

All flesh is grass.   *Isaiah* xl, *c.* 700 B.C.

"All flesh," says Paul, "is not the same flesh. There
is one flesh of men; another of beasts; another of
fishes; and another of birds." And what then?—
nothing. A cook could have said as much.

THOMAS PAINE, 1737-1809, *The Age of Reason*

A meal without flesh is like feeding on grass.

BHOJPURI PROVERB

The horse bit the parson!
   How came it to pass?
The horse heard the parson say,
   "All flesh is grass."

H. J. LOARING, *Epitaphs Quaint, Curious and Elegant*, 1872

These are the beasts which we shall eat; the ox, the
sheep, and the goat.   *Deuteronomy* xiv, 4, *c.* 520 B.C.

What say you to a piece of beef and mustard?

WILLIAM SHAKESPEARE, 1564-1616, *The Taming of the Shrew*

Oh! The roast beef of England,
And old England's roast beef.

HENRY FIELDING, 1707-1754, *Grub Street Opera*

Pudding and beef make Britons fight.

MATTHEW PRIOR, 1664-1721, *Alma*

And as for excellent good Beef and Veale, there is no
countrie in the world that can parallel, farre less
exceed our beeves and veale here in England, whatsoever some talke of Hungary and Poland.

HART, *The Diet of the Diseased*, 1633

Methinks sometimes I have no more wit than a
Christian or an ordinary man has; but I am a great
eater of beef, and I believe that does harm to my wit.

WILLIAM SHAKESPEARE, 1564-1616, *Twelfth Night*

Any of us would kill a cow rather than not have beef.

SAMUEL JOHNSON, 1709-1784

But no doubt the first man that ever murdered an ox
was regarded as a murderer; perhaps he was hung;
and if he had been put on trial by oxen, he certainly
would have been; and he certainly deserved it if any
murderer does. Go to the meatmarket of a Saturday
night and see the crowds of live bipeds staring up at
the long rows of dead quadrupeds. Does not that
sight take a tooth out of the cannibal's jaw? Cannibals? Who is not a cannibal? I tell you it will be more
tolerable for the Fejee that salted down a lean missionary in his cellar against a coming famine; it will
be more tolerable for that provident Fejee, I say, in
the day of judgment, than for thee, civilized and

enlightened gourmand, who naileth geese to the
ground and feasteth on their bloated livers in thy
paté-de-foie-gras.

HERMAN MELVILLE, 1819-1891, *Moby Dick*

Talk of joy: there may be things better than beef
stew and baked potatoes and home-made bread—
there may be.

DAVID GRAYSON, 1870-1946, *Adventures in Contentment*

I think I could eat one of Bellamy's veal pies.

WILLIAM PITT, 1759-1806, Attributed last words

. . . every one knows that some young bucks among
the epicures, by continually dining upon calves'
brains, by and by get to have a little brains of their
own, so as to be able to tell a calf's head from their
own heads; which, indeed, requires uncommon dis-
crimination. And that is why a young buck with a
calf's head before him, is somehow one of the oddest
sights you can see. The head looks sort of reproach-
fully at him, with an "Et tu Brute!" expression.

HERMAN MELVILLE, 1819-1891, *Moby Dick*

The young wild boar, known in French as a *marcas-
sin*, and in hunting terms as a *bête rousse*, may be prepared in every way the same as a full-grown boar.
In olden times, hunters never killed them, but, having caught them, castrated them and let them loose.
Thus "perfected" as they say of the choir boys in

the Sistine Chapel, they grow bigger, more delicate, and less wild.

Babirusa: A sort of wild boar only recently seen in Europe. There are specimens in the Jardin des Plantes. Pliny said of it: "In the Indies there is a sort of wild boar that has two horns like a calf's and tusks like an ordinary wild boar."

"Good Lord, darling!" said a lady to her husband at the zoo. "What is that animal that has four horns instead of two?"

"Madam," said a bystander, "it's a widower who has remarried."

. . . The flesh is very pleasing to the taste. He is eaten like a wild boar.

Bear meat is now eaten everywhere in Europe. From the most ancient times, the front paws have been regarded as the most delicate morsel.

ALEXANDRE DUMAS, 1802-1870, *Dictionary of Cuisine*

I have been assured by a very knowing American of my acquaintance in London that a young healthy child, well nursed, is at a year old a most delicious, nourishing and wholesome food, whether stewed, roasted, baked or boiled; and I make no doubt that it will equally serve in a fricasee or ragout.

JONATHAN SWIFT, 1667-1745, *A Modest Proposal* . . .

Give a dog an appetizing name and eat him.

CHINESE PROVERB

The fox, when caught, is worth nothing: he is followed for the pleasure of following.

SYDNEY SMITH, 1771-1845

The English country gentleman galloping after a fox
—the unspeakable in full pursuit of the uneatable.

OSCAR WILDE, 1856-1900,
A Woman of No Importance

At this moment I bit into one of my frankfurters, and—Christ!

I can't honestly say that I'd expected the thing to have a pleasant taste. I'd expected it to taste of nothing, like the roll. But this—well, it was quite an experience. Let me try and describe it to you.

The frankfurter had a rubber skin, of course, and my temporary teeth weren't much of a fit. I had to do a kind of sawing movement before I could get my teeth through the skin. And then suddenly—pop! The thing burst in my mouth like a rotten pear. A sort of horrible soft stuff was oozing over my tongue. But the taste! For a moment I just couldn't believe it! Then I rolled my tongue around it again and had another try. It was fish! A sausage, a thing calling itself a frankfurter filled with fish! I got up and walked straight out without touching my coffee. God knows what that might have tasted of. . . . It gave me the feeling that I'd bitten into the modern world and discovered what it was really made of.

GEORGE ORWELL, 1903-1950, *Coming Up for Air*

I have been in France, and have eaten frogs. The nicest little rabbity things you ever tasted.
CHARLES LAMB, 1775-1834, Letter to John Clare

I marvel why frogs and snails are with some people, and in some countries, in great account, and judged wholesome food, whereas indeed they have in them nothing else but a cold, gross, slimy and excremental juice.   TOBIAS VENNER, 1577-1660, *Via recta ad vitam longam*

Giraffe are splendid eating, and in good condition and fat are a luxury that no one can properly appreciate till he has lived for a time on nothing but the dry meat of the smaller antelopes.
FREDERICK COURTENEY SELOUS, 1851-1917,
A Hunter's Wanderings in Africa

Even these . . . ye may eat: the grasshopper after his kind.   *Leviticus* xi, 22, *c*. 700 B.C.

As mad as a March hare.   ENGLISH PROVERB

Take your hare when it is cased.
[Usually misquoted as "First catch your hare."]
HANNAH GLASSE, fl. 1747, *The Art of Cookery*

Hare, a black meat, is melancholy and hard of digestion. ROBERT BURTON, 1577-1640, *Anatomy of Melancholy*

Horseflesh has never been popular in the British Isles,

but it has long been in demand on the Continent. The fillet of a three-year-old thoroughbred is a costly luxury, but it is a very good meat indeed: one has no chance of tasting it unless the horse happens to break its neck at exercise or otherwise injures itself so badly that it has to be destroyed. The majority of horse-flesh sold by horse butchers is sound and wholesome meat, but too muscular to be enjoyable: it usually comes from horses too old for work as well as too old to roast: it is best boiled, stewed or in pies. . . .

On February 29th, 1868 a horseflesh dinner was served at the Langham Hotel in London, and Frank Buckland who was invited to it, said that he "gave it a fair trial, tasting every dish from soup to jelly," but he did not approve of any of it.

Concise Encyclopaedia of Gastronomy, 1945

In the U.S.A., mutton is not mentioned at all in polite culinary society; one never gets anything but lamb.   *Concise Encyclopaedia of Gastronomy*, 1945

Of all birds, give me mutton.

THOMAS FULLER, 1608-1661, *Gnomologia*

The leg of mutton of Wales beats the leg of mutton of any other country.

GEORGE BORROW, 1803-1881, *Wild Wales*

The mountain sheep are sweeter,
  But the valley sheep are fatter;

We therefore deemed it meeter
  To carry off the latter.
                              THOMAS LOVE PEACOCK, 1785-1866,
                                  The Misfortunes of Elphin

Mutton: It is as bad as bad can be: it is ill-fed, ill-
killed, ill-kept, and ill-drest.
                              SAMUEL JOHNSON, 1709-1784,
                                  On the roast mutton he had for dinner

Flesh of a mutton is food for a glutton.
          RANDLE COTGRAVE, d. 1634?, *French-English Dictionary*

The flesh of the moose is very good; though some
deem it coarse. Old hunters, who always like rich,
greasy food, rank a moose's nose with a beaver's
tail, as the chief of backwood delicacies; personally
I never liked either.   THEODORE ROOSEVELT, 1858-1919,
          Big Game Hunting in the Rockies and on the Great Plains

Ham is generally not half soaked, as salt as Brine,
and as hard as Flint; and it would puzzle the stomach
of an Ostrich to digest it.
                              THOMAS LOVE PEACOCK, 1785-1866

Kill a pig and eat a year; kill an ox and eat a week.
                              CHINESE PROVERB

Even fat pigs give much lean meat.
                              PORTUGUESE PROVERB

Fresh pork and new wine bring an early death.

SPANISH PROVERB

The hog is never good but when he is in the dish.

LEONARD MASCALL, *The Book of Cattle*, 1587

A Tartar does not eat pig, because he is a pig himself.

RUSSIAN PROVERB

Of pigs don't eat the liver or the blood; of fishes do not eat either shrimps or turtle.   CHINESE PROVERB

Neither is all swines' flesh so commendable, but that which is young and best of a yeare or two old. Also better of a wilde swine than of a tame.

HENRY COGAN, fl. 1650, *The Haven of Helth*

Once or twice a year every cottager ought to kill a pig. If a pig is washed and kept clean, it softens the skin and allows it to expand; in fact, a pig thus treated comes much quicker round; it is proved that a pig at fourteen months, kept clean, is equal to one at eighteen which is not attended to.

ALEXIS SOYER, 1809-1858,
A Shilling Cookery for the People

There was lately a man that, if pork, or anything made of swine's flesh, were brought into the room, he would fall into a convulsive, sardonic laughter; nor can he for his heart leave as long as that object

is before him, so that, if it should be not removed,
he would certainly laugh himself to death.

INCREASE MATHER, 1639-1723, *Remarkable Providences*

In converting Jews to Christians, you raise the price
of pork.

WILLIAM SHAKESPEARE, 1564-1616, *The Merchant of Venice*

Everything has an end, except a sausage, which has
two.   DANISH PROVERB

Bologna is celebrated for producing popes, painters,
and sausages.

LORD BYRON, 1788-1824, Letter to John Murray

Stuffed with a simple stuffing made of bread crumbs,
a sprinkling of sweet herbs, and a little pepper and
salt, mixed with the liver and heart of the rat, and
roasted for a few minutes in a hot oven, it proved to
be a delicious dish not unlike a snipe in flavour. Young
rats may also be made into pies, if meat stock, Bovril
or a small piece of beef be added to provide the gravy.

L. C. CAMERON, *The Wild Foods of Great Britain*

Why is not a rat as good as a rabbit? Why should
men eat shrimps and neglect cockroaches?

H. W. BEECHER, 1813-1887, *Eyes and Ears*

How say you to a fat tripe finely broiled?

WILLIAM SHAKESPEARE, 1564-1616, *The Taming of the Shrew*

Tripe's good meat if it be well wiped.

JOHN RAY, 1627-1705, *English Proverbs*

. . . So home and dined there with my wife upon a most excellent dish of tripes of my own directing, covered with mustard, as I have seen them heretofore done at my Lord Crewe's; of which I made a very great meal and sent for a glass of wine for myself.

SAMUEL PEPYS, 1633-1703, *Diary*

I have known a human defended from strong temptations to social ambitions by a still stronger taste for tripe and onions. C. S. LEWIS, 1898-1963, *The Screwtape Letters*

Save when at noon his paunch grew mutinous
For a plate of turtle green and glutinous.

ROBERT BROWNING, 1812-1889, *The Pied Piper of Hamelin*

The diamond-backed [terrapin] is a handsome reptile, whose meat, when properly stewed, is tender gelatinous. Gastronomically, it is by far the finest of the North American turtles, and terrapin stew is our costliest native delicacy. . . .

". . . Eat enough of it and it'll make an old rooster out of you. Why do you think so many rich old men eat terrapin? Well, sir, I'll tell you why. A terrapin is loaded down with a rich, nourishing jelly, and this jelly makes you feel young again. To be frank, it's the same as monkey glands. If you were to take and feed terrapin stew to all the people of this country, the birth rate would like a flash of lightning. . . ."

. . . The three of us sat down and while we ate Mrs.
Barbee gave me a list of the things in the stew. She
said it contained the meat, hearts, and livers of two
diamond-backs killed early that day, eight yolks of
hard-boiled eggs that had been pounded up and
passed through a sieve, a half pound of yellow country butter, two pints of thick cream, a little flour, a
pinch of salt, a dash of nutmeg, and a glass and a
half of amontillado. The meat came off terrapin's
tiny bones with a touch of the spoon, and it tasted
like delicate baby mushrooms.

JOSEPH MITCHELL, in *McSorley's Wonderful Saloon*, 1943

The whale that wanders round the Pole
Is not a table fish.
You cannot bake or boil him whole
Nor serve him in a dish.

HILAIRE BELLOC, 1870-1953, *Bad Child's Book of Beasts*

. . . Stubb was a high liver; he was somewhat in-
temperately fond of the whale as a flavorish thing
to his palate.

"A steak, a steak, ere I sleep! You, Daggoo! over-
board you go, and cut me one from his small!"

Here be it known, that though these wild fishermen do not, as a general thing, and according to the
great military maxim, make the enemy defray the
current expenses of the war (at least before realizing
the proceeds of the voyage), yet now and then you
find some of these Nantucketeers who have a genuine

relish for that particular part of the Sperm Whale designated by Stubb; comprising the tapering extremity of the body.

About midnight that steak was cut and cooked; and lighted by two lanterns of sperm oil, Stubb stoutly stood up to his spermacetti supper at the capstan-head, as if that capstan were a sideboard.

. . . "Cook," said Stubb, rapidly lifting a rather reddish morsel to his mouth, "don't you think this steak is rather overdone? You've been beating this steak too much, cook; it's too tender. Don't I always say that to be good, a whale-steak must be tough?"

"Well then, cook, you see this whale-steak of yours was so very bad, that I have put it out of sight as soon as possible; you see that, don't you? Well, for the future, when you cook another whale-steak for my private table here, the capstan, I'll tell you what to do so as not to spoil it by overdoing. Hold the steak in one hand, and show a live coal to it with the other; that done, dish it; d'ye hear? And now to-morrow, cook, when we are cutting in the fish, be sure you stand by to get the tips of his fins; have them put in pickle. As for the ends of the flukes, have them soused, cook. There, now ye may go. . . ."

That mortal man should feed upon the creature that feeds his lamp, and, like Stubb, eat him by his own light, as you may say; this seems so outlandish a thing that one must needs go a little into the history and philosophy of it.

It is upon record, that three centuries ago the

tongue of the Right Whale was esteemed a great
delicacy in France, and commanded large prices there.
Also, that in Henry VIII's time, a certain cook of the
court obtained a handsome reward for inventing an
admirable sauce to be eaten with barbecued porpoises, which, you remember, are a species of whale.

The fact is, that among his hunters at least, the
whale would by all hands be considered a noble dish,
were there not so much of him; but when you come
to sit down before a meat-pie nearly one hundred feet
long, it takes away your appetite. Only the most un-
prejudiced of men like Stubb, nowadays partake of
cooked whales; but the Esquimaux are not so fastidi-
ous. We all know how they live upon whales, and
have rare old vintages of prime old train oil. Zog-
randa, one of their most famous doctors, recommends strips of blubber for infants, as being exceedingly juicy and nourishing. . . .

But what further depreciates the whale as a civilized dish, is his exceeding richness. He is the great
prize ox of the sea, too fat to be delicately good.
Look at his hump, which would be as fine eating as
the buffalo's (which is esteemed a rare dish), were
it not such a solid pyramid of fat. But the spermacetti itself, how bland and creamy that is; like the
transparent, half-jellied white meat of the cocoanut
in the third month of its growth, yet far too rich
to supply a substitute for butter. Nevertheless, many
whalemen have a method of absorbing it into some
other substance, and then partaking of it. In the

long dry watches of the night it is a common thing
for the seamen to dip their ship-biscuit into the huge
oil-pots and let them fry there for a while. Many a
good supper have I thus made. . . .

It is not, perhaps, entirely because the whale is
so excessively unctuous that landsmen seem to regard
the eating of him with abhorrence; that appears to
result, in some way, from the consideration before
mentioned: i.e. that a man should eat a newly murdered thing of the sea, and eat it too by its own
light. . . .

But Stubb, he eats the whale by its own light, does
he? and that is adding insult to injury, is it? Look at
your own knife-handle, there, my civilized and enlightened gourmand dining off that roast beef, what
is that handle made of?—what but the bones of the
brother of the very ox you are eating? And what do
you pick your teeth with after devouring that fat
goose? with a feather of the same fowl. And with
what quill did the Secretary of the Society for the
Suppression of Cruelty to Ganders formally indite
his circulars? It is only within the last month or two
that that society passed a resolution to patronize
nothing but steel pens.

                    HERMAN MELVILLE, 1819-1891, *Moby Dick*

Zebra: The flesh is generally loaded with a yellow
fat, and is very unpalatable to Europeans, but by the
African natives it is regarded as a great delicacy.

                    W. L. SLATER, *Mammals of South Africa*

o*f* VEGETABLES

ℛAIN is good for vegetables, and for animals who eat those vegetables, and for the animals who eat those animals.   SAMUEL JOHNSON, 1709-1784, Boswell's *Life*

Persons living entirely on vegetables are seldom of a plump and succulent habit.

WILLIAM CULLEN, 1710-1790,
First Lines of the Practise of Physic

Vegetarians have wicked, shifty eyes, and laugh in a cold and calculating manner. They pinch little children, steal stamps, drink water, favour beards . . . wheeze, squeak, drawl and maunder.

J. B. MORTON, 1893- , *By the Way*

There is no disease, bodily or mental, which adoption of vegetable diet and pure water has not infallibly mitigated, wherever the experiment has been fairly tried.

PERCY BYSSHE SHELLEY, 1792-1822, Queen Mab, Notes

Carthusian of Meat and Vegetables. You will perhaps be surprised at the name I have given to this curious mixture of vegetable produce, but you will immediately perceive I have taken it from those well known monks who took vows to partake of no animal food, something like our strict vegetarians of the present day; but these jolly old dogs in former days were obliged, at times, to break their vows; as, however it could not be done openly, they were obliged to mask the object cooked in a covering of vegetables, and thus cheated their oath and their conscience.

Carthusian, or Chartreuse, in French cookery, means any article of food, such as meat, game, or poultry, so surrounded by vegetables, that even a vegetarian would be deceived with its appearance, while sitting at dinner, and would not find out his mistake until helped with some of the dishes.

ALEXIS SOYER, 1809-1858,
A Shilling Cookery for the People

I have a friend, a vegetarian seer,
By name Elias Baptist Butterworth,
A harmless, bland disinterested man.

GEORGE ELIOT, 1819-1880, A Minor Prophet

My digestion is weak; I am too bilious to eat more than once a day, and generally live on vegetables. To be sure I drink two bottles of wine at dinner, but they form only a vegetable diet. Just now I live on claret and soda-water.   THOMAS MEDWIN, 1788-1869,
Journal of the Conversation of Lord Byron

But it is best to eate the Artichoke boyled; the ribbes of the leaves are altogether of an hard substance: they yeeld to the body a raw and melancholy juyce, and containe in them great store of winde.
                        JOHN GERARD, 1545-1612, *Herball*

Among this month's [September] vegetables one must include the autumn artichokes, remarkable for their delicacy and good taste. The best come from Laon and are easy to select, being always carefully packed for the journey—this vegetable being rather delicate. Large artichokes are served boiled and are to be eaten with a very fine butter sauce or with oil, prepared this way one must agree they make a respectable side dish. Small and middle-size ones, which are no less tender, lend themselves to such a variety of treatments, that in the hands of a knowledgeable artist they take on a chameleon-like quality. They may be eaten with Spanish sauce, au jus, in chicken stew, fried, etc. . . .

The artichoke gives, as one can see, distinguished service in the kitchen; one can scarcely be without it, and when it is not to be had it is truly a calamity.

We should add that it is a very healthful food;
nourishing, a tonic for the stomach, astringent, and
slightly aphrodisiacal. It is a dish which agrees with
people of weak stomachs, consequently with men of
letters; but it is only good for them cooked, they
should avoid it like poison when raw because then
its acidity and astringent qualities can cause a great
deal of harm. It should also be said these sort of
people should absolutely abstain from spiced artichokes which only agree with vulgar stomachs.

GRIMOD DE LA REYNIERE,
Almanach des Gourmands, 1803

The bare naked tender shoots of Sperage spring up
in Aprill, at what time they are eaten in sallads;
they floure in June and July, the fruit is ripe in
September.

It is named Asparagus, of the excellency, because
asparagi, or the springs hereof are preferred before
those of other plants whatsoever: for their Latine
word *Asparagus* doth properly signifie the first spring
or sprout of every plant, especially when it is tender,
and before it do grow into an hard stalk, as are the
buds, tendrels, or yong springs of wild Vine or hops,
and such like.

The first sprouts or naked tender shoots hereof be
oftentimes sodden in flesh broth and eaten; or boiled
in faire water, and seasoned with oile, vinegar, salt,
and pepper, then are served up as a sallad; they are
pleasant to the taste.   JOHN GERARD, 1545-1607, *Herball*

Sparagus, *Asparagus* (*ab Aspiritate*) temperately hot, and moist; Cordial, Diuretic, easie of Digestion, and next to Flesh, nothing more nourishing, as Sim. Sethius, an excellent Physician, holds. They are sometimes, but very seldom, eaten raw with Oyl, and Vinegar; but with more delicacy (the bitterness first exhausted) being so speedily boil'd as not to lose the *verdure* and agreeable tenderness; which is done by letting the Water boil, before you put them in. I do not esteem the Dutch great and larger sort (especially rais'd by the rankness of the Beds) so sweet and agreeable, as those of a moderate size.

JOHN EVELYN, 1620-1706, *Acetaria*

Asparagus: There are three varieties, white, violet, and green. The white is the earliest. Its flavour is mild and pleasant, but it has little substance. The violet is the thickest and most substantial. The green is thinner, but more of it is edible. It has a fine flavour. In Italy where taste is stronger than refined, the wild asparagus is preferred. The best way to prepare asparagus is by steaming. The Romans had a saying when they wanted something done quickly. "Do it," they said, "in less time than it takes to cook asparagus." ALEXANDRE DUMAS, 1802-1870

At the end of this month [April] one sees the points of asparagus emerge, something which brings a great consolation to those who, tired of potatoes and dried cereals, long for something green.

This vegetable, always dear in Paris, and only seemly for the rich because it is not very substantial and somewhat aphrodisiacal, is a very delicate food. The large stalks, cooked in water, are served to be eaten either with a white sauce or with oil. The small ones are served like peas to deceive our hopes and calm our impatience. But so soon as real peas come in one does not dare present them in this guise. It is thus that a beauty with the aid of fine lighting, having stolen our praises flees at the prospect of dawn for she dares not risk comparison with an Hebe of just eighteen springs.

GRIMOD DE LA REYNIERE, *Almanach des Gourmands*, 1803

The green and gold of my delight—
Asparagus with Hollandaise!

THOMAS AUGUSTINE DALY, 1871-1948, *Ballade by Glutton*

Abstain from beans. *Abstineo a fabis*. Taverner (1539) states: "There be sondry interpretacions of this symbole. But Plutarche and Cicero thynke beanes to be forbydden of Pythagoras, because they be wyndye and do engender impure humours and for that cause provoke bodely lust."   LATIN PROVERB

Beans are eaten green in their pods; mature, with the pods removed when they are called *flageolets*; and dried, when they are called Soissons beans, no matter where they come from. Since I am from the department of Aisne, I must necessarily appreciate my compatriots, and, in fact, until my last visit to Asia I would have said that beans actually from Soissons were the best in the world. But I feel obliged to recognize the fact that beans from Trebizon are better.   ALEXANDRE DUMAS, 1802-1870

There is no dignity in the bean. Corn, with no affectation of superiority, is, however, the child of song. It waves in all literature. But mix it with beans, and its high tone is gone. Succotash is vulgar.
    CHARLES DUDLEY WARNER, 1829-1900, *My Summer in a Garden*

And this is good old Boston,
The home of the bean and the cod,
Where the Lowells talk to the Cabots,
And the Cabots talk only to God.
                          J. C. BOSSIDY, 1860-1928,
                Toast proposed at a Harvard dinner

Full o' beans and benevolence.
                R. S. SURTEES, 1803-1869, *Handley Cross*

Shake a Leicestershire-man by the collar, and you shall hear the beans rattle in his belly.
              THOMAS FULLER, 1608-1661, *Gnomologia*

There will be no beans in the Almost Perfect State.
        DON MARQUIS, 1878-1937, *The Almost Perfect State*

Beet: This plant contains more sugar than any other.

At the time of the Continental blockade the chemists conceived the idea of substituting beet for sugar
cane. I can remember seeing, in 1812, a caricature
showing the King of Rome with his nurse. The
child was crying, and his nurse was offering him a
beet, saying, "Suck it, my child, your father says it
is sugar." As with all great discoveries, this one
that freed us from dependence on the colonies was
greeted with derision. The people who worshipped
Napoleon so long for his victories, which cost a
third of our blood and a sixth of our territory, do not
dream that they owe beet sugar to him.

ALEXANDRE DUMAS, 1802-1870

Beet: Being eaten when it is boyled, it nourishes
little or nothing, and is not so wholesome as Lettuce.
    The juyce conveighed up into the nostrils doth
gently draw forth flegme, and purgeth the head.
    The greater red Beet or Roman Beet, boyled and
eaten with oyle, vinegre and pepper, is a most excellent and delicat sallad: but what might be made of
the red and beautifull root (which is to be preferred
before the leaves, as well in beautie as in goodnesse)
I refer unto the curious and cunning cooke, who no
doubt when hee had the view thereof, and is assured
that it is both good and wholesome, will make many
and diverse dishes, both faire and good.

JOHN GERARD, 1545-1607, *Herball*

The beetroot is a better emblem of modesty than the

rose. The colour is as fine; it conceals itself from the view more completely; moreover it is good to eat, and will make excellent sugar.

SAMUEL BUTLER, 1612-1680, *Notebooks*

Cabbage: A familiar kitchen-garden vegetable about as large and wise as a man's head.

AMBROSE BIERCE, 1842-?1914, *The Devil's Dictionary*

There are various types of cabbages, nearly all of them originating in Europe, where they are most widely used. In nearly every French province cabbage is the mainstay of the peasants, who live chiefly on this vegetable, even though it has little nourishment, is windy, and spreads an evil odour. Cabbage was greatly venerated by the ancients, who swore by it just as the Egyptians rendered divine honours to the onion.

ALEXANDRE DUMAS, 1802-1870

Cabbages are a great help in the kitchen—even in the kitchens of the knowing. A clever chef knows how to take advantage of this plant to give variety to his soups, garnitures, etc. We have seen a beef culotte and even a grown partridge holding it an honor to be flanked by a thick wall of cabbage. Everything depends on the seasoning. It is thus that the most vulgar phrases are ennobled by the pen of a great poet. Bavarian cabbage, as the preferred base of chitterlings, is not at all an ordinary stew.

GRIMOD DE LA REYNIERE, *Almanach des Gourmands*, 1803

In our precious cabbage patches the holometabolous insecta are the hosts of parasitic polyembryonic hymenoptera, upon the prevalence of which rests the psychic somatic stamina of our fellow-countrymen.
WILLIAM OSLER, 1849-1919, Address before the Classical Association at Oxford, May 16, 1919

There was a shortage of broccoli, aubergines, turnips and watercress, which he meant to raise in a trough. After the thaw, all the artichokes perished. The cabbages consoled him. One in particular filled him with hope. It spread out, grew still taller, and ended by being colossal and quite inedible. No matter, Pécuchet was happy to possess a prodigy.
GUSTAVE FLAUBERT, 1821-1880, Bouvard and Pécuchet

The gardener's dog neither eats cabbage himself nor lets anyone else eat it.   FRENCH PROVERB

Cabbage twice cooked is death.   GREEK PROVERB

It is the reproduction of the cabbage that wears out the master's life. [i.e. twice cooked]
JUVENAL, c. 60-130, Satires

The only way to keep a family in existence for generations is to think cabbage-stalks nice.
CHINESE PROVERB

Cauliflower is nothing but cabbage with a college education.   MARK TWAIN, 1835-1910, Pudd'nhead Wilson

Cauliflower: Nonetheless healthy than spinach, it offers less trouble in its preparation—and without being very clever, a cook can prepare for your eating excellent dishes of cauliflower in white sauce, with mutton gravy, fried in patties, with parmesan cheese —which are the most appetizing ways of serving them. Cauliflower is also served with an entourage for many dishes and as a garniture in many ragouts; even salads are made with it. And, after all, it is a very pretty vegetable and lends itself beautifully to the decoration of a table. One should choose cauliflower with firm, white heads—those with dirty white, grained heads should be rejected.

GRIMOD DE LA REYNIERE,
Almanach des Gourmands, 1803

Sellery, *Apium Italicum*, (and of the *Petroselene* Family) was formerly a stranger with us (nor very long since in *Italy*) is an hot and more generous sort of *Macedonian Persley*, or *Smallage*. The tender leaves of the *Blancht* Stalk do well in our Sallet, as likewise the slices of the whiten'd Stems, which being crimp and short, first peel'd and slit long wise, are eaten with *Oyl*, *Vinegar*, *Salt*, and *Peper*; and for its high and grateful Taste, is ever plac'd in the middle of the *Grand Sallet*, at our Great Mens Tables, and *Praetors* Feasts, as the Grace of the whole Board. *Caution* is to be given of a small red Worm, often lurking in these Stalks, as does the green in *Fennil*.

JOHN EVELYN, 1620-1706, *Acetaria*

Celery: The first that I ever saw was in a Venetian
Ambassador's garden in the spittle yard, near Bish-
op's Gate Street. The first year it is planted with us
it is sweete and pleasant, especially while it is young,
but after it has grown high and large hath a stronger
taste of smallage, and so much more the following
yeare. The Venetians used to prepare it for meate
many waies, bothe the herbe and roote eaten rawe,
or boyled or fryed to be eaten with meate; but most
usually either whited and so eaten rawe with pepper
and oyle as a dainty sallet of itselfe, or a little
boyled or stewed . . . the taste of the herbe being a
little warming, but the seede much more.

JOHN PARKINSON, 1567-1650, *Paradisus Terrestris*

Celery: In small households one uses it for an eco-
nomical dish prepared like chard, but the noblest
way it may be placed on our tables, is creamed; a
well-made creamed celery honors a good cook as
much as it offers great difficulties.

Though celery, after it is cooked, loses many of
its medicinal qualities, one for all that, cannot deny
that it is an aromatic, digestive, appetizing, warming, and consequently rather importantly, aphrodisiacal plant. We are obliged, to assuage our conscience,
to warn timid people of this last quality of celery, so
they can abstain from it, or be prudent in its use.
That is to say that it is *not* a salad for bachelors.

GRIMOD DE LA REYNIERE,
Almanach des Gourmands, 1803

The Cucumber is named generally *Cucumis*: in shops
Cucumer: in English Cowcumbers and Cucumbers.

The fruit cut in pieces or chopped as herbes to the
pot and boiled in a small pipkin with a piece of
mutton, being made into potage with Ote-meale, even
as herb potage are made, whereof a messe to breakfast, as much to dinner, and the like to supper; taken
in this manner for the space of three weekes together
without intermission, doth perfectly cure all manner
of sauce flegme and copper faces, red and shining
fierie noses (as red as red Roses) with pimples, pum-
ples, rubies, and such like precious faces.

JOHN GERARD, 1545-1607, Herball

It is almost sure death to eat cucumbers and drink
milk at the same meal.   H. L. MENCKEN, 1880-1956 &
GEORGE JEAN NATHAN, 1882-1958, American Credo

As cold as cucumbers.
BEAUMONT, 1584-1616, & FLETCHER, 1579-1625, Cupid's Revenge

A scarecrow in a garden of cucumbers keepeth
nothing.   <i>Apocrypha: Baruch</i> vi, 70

The leek is the most modest of these four [also carrots, onions, turnips] kitchen-garden vegetables; it
never appears on our tables except in soup to which
it adds a good savor; it is used in the same way
added to the *bouquet garni* in stews or ragouts: it is a
very healthful vegetable and can play a more notice-

able part as a garniture—a thought we leave for
those in the art.
        GRIMOD DE LA REYNIERE, *Almanach des Gourmands*, 1803

I hate with a bitter hatred the names of lentils hari-
cots—those pretentious cheats of the appetite, those
tabulated humbugs, those certified aridities calling
themselves human food!   GEORGE GISSING, 1857-1903

Well loved he garleek, oynons, and eek lekes,
And for to drinken strong wyn, reed as blood.
        GEOFFREY CHAUCER, 1340?-1400, *Canterbury Tales*

The Onions do bite, attenuate or make thin, and
cause drynesse: being boiled they do lose their sharpnesse, especially if the water be twice or thrice
changed, and yet for all that they do lose their at-
tenuating qualitie.

The juice of Onions snuffed up into the nose,
purgeth the head, and draweth forth raw flegmatic
humors. Stamped with Salt, Roe, and Honey, and so
applied, they are good against the biting of a mad
Dog. Rosted in the embers and applied, they ripen
and breake cold Apostumes, Biles, and such like.

The juice of Onions mixed with the decoction of
Penniroyall, and anointed upon the goutie member
with a feather, or a cloth wet therein, and applied,
easeth the same very much. The juice anointed upon
a pild or bald head in the Sun, bringeth the haire
againe very speedily.

. . . Onions sliced and dipped in the juice of Sorrell, and given unto the Sicke of a tertian Ague, to eat, takes away the fit in once or twice so taking them.

The Onion being eaten, yea though it be boiled, causeth head-ache, hurteth the eyes, and maketh a man dim sighted, dulleth the sences, and provoketh overmuch sleep, especially being eaten raw.

JOHN GERARD, 1545-1607

Happy is said to be the family which can eat onions together. They are, for the time being, separate from the world, and have a harmony of aspiration.

CHARLES DUDLEY WARNER, 1829-1900,
My Summer in a Garden

For this is every cook's opinion,
No savoury dish without an onion;
But lest your kissing should be spoiled,
Your onions must be thoroughly boiled.

JONATHAN SWIFT, 1667-1745

Eat no onions or garlic, for we are to utter sweet breath.

WILLIAM SHAKESPEARE, 1564-1616, *A Midsummer Night's Dream*

How beautiful and strong those buttered onions come to my nose!

CHARLES LAMB, 1775-1834, Letter to Thomas Manning

It will do with an onion.   ENGLISH PROVERB

If thou hast not a capon feed on an onion.

ENGLISH PROVERB

He liked to get a whole onion in the hollowed out heel of a loaf of French bread and eat it as if it were an apple. He had an extraordinary appetite for onions, the stronger the better, and said that "Good ale, raw onions, and no ladies" was the motto of his saloon.   JOSEPH MITCHELL describing John McSorley
in *McSorley's Wonderful Saloon*, 1943

Where hearts were high and fortunes low, and onions in the stew.

CHARLES DIVINE, 1889-1950, *At the Lavender Lantern*

Let onion atoms lurk within the bowl,
And, half-suspected, animate the whole.

SYDNEY SMITH, 1771-1845

The play left a taste of lukewarm parsnip juice.

ALEXANDER WOOLLCOTT, 1887-1943

It groweth naturally in America, where it was first discovered, as reporteth *Clusius*, since which time roots hereof from Virginia, otherwise called Norimbega, which grow and prosper in my garden as in their own native country.

The Indians call this plant Pappus, meaning the roots; by which name also the common Potatoes are called in these Indian countries. . . .

The vertues be referred to the common Potato's,
being likewise a food, as also a meat for pleasure,
equall in goodnesse and wholesomeness to the same,
being either rooted in the embers, or boiled and eaten
with oile, vineger and pepper, or dressed some other
way by the hand of a skilfull cooke.

> JOHN GERARD, 1545-1607, *Herball*

Only two things in this world are too serious to be
jested on—potatoes and matrimony.   IRISH APHORISM

Pray for peace and grace and spiritual food,
For wisdom and guidance, for all these are good,
But don't forget the potatoes.

> JOHN TYLER PETTEE, 1822-1907, *Prayer and Potatoes*

The best part of a potato is underground.

> ENGLISH SAYING not recorded before 19th century

A hot potato is hard to cool.   AMERICAN PROVERB

An attachment à la Plato for a bashful young potato, or a not-too-French French bean.

> W. S. GILBERT, 1836-1911, *Patience*

The French fried potato has become an inescapable
horror in almost every public eating place in the
country. "French fries," say the menus, but they are
not French fries any longer. They are a furry-textured
substance with the taste of plastic wood.

> RUSSELL BAKER, in *New York Times*, Feb. 22, 1968

If fresh meat be wanting to fill up our dish
We have carrots and pumpkins and turnips and fish;
We have pumpkins at morning and pumpkins at noon;
If it was not for pumpkins we should be undone.

ANONYMOUS, *New England Annoyances*, 1630

When the rice is not well cooked it is because the steam has been unequally distributed.

CHINESE PROVERB

In China we have only three religions, but we have a hundred dishes we can make from rice.

CHINESE PROVERB

Thunder will not strike when eating rice.

CHINESE PROVERB

Rice is the best food for the soldier.

NAPOLEON I, 1769-1821,
To Gaspar Gourgaud at St. Helena

Finally, everywhere in Germany, and even in Alsace, they make, with fermented red cabbage, a dish known as sauerkraut, which in causing the cabbage to lose its deleterious qualities, produces a food as healthful as it is agreeable and a good reserve supply for the winter for use either as a main course or a garniture. For a few years now [1803] sauerkraut has been accepted in Paris.

GRIMOD DE LA REYNIERE, *Almanach des Gourmands*, 1803

Sauerkraut is good for a cold.   GERMAN PROVERB

Spinach, *Spinachia*: of old not us'd in *Sallets*, and the
oftener kept out the better; I speak of the *crude*: But
being boil'd to a *Pult*, and without other Water than
its own moisture, is a most excellent Condiment with
Butter, Vinegar, or Limon, for almost all sorts of
boil'd Flesh, and may accompany a Sick Man's Diet.
'Tis *Laxative* and *Emollient*, and therefore profitable
for the Aged, and (tho' by original a Spaniard) may
be had at almost any Season, and in all places.

JOHN EVELYN, 1620-1706, *Acetaria*

Though the vegetable is easily available, it is nevertheless equally the despair of the stingy and industrious, because its preparation can be costly and difficult, above all when one takes full advantage of its
great possibilities. Spinach is worthy in itself, it is
like sealing wax, available to receive all impressions,
but in the hands of a skillful cook it can attain great
worth. A fine dish of spinach by itself, has made a
cook's reputation.

Spinach, the healthiest of vegetables, agreeable
to all stomachs, lends itself to cooking with meats,
butter, cream, or gravy; with it one can make soups,
pies, risolés; it can serve as an accompaniment to
distinguished dishes: and it is, after sorrel, the usual
bed for stewed meats: it is always served with tongue
and the sliced smoked beef of Hambourg. Finally, it
is the mainstay of the poor man's table, as it is the

glory of that of the rich: everything depends on the hands through which it passes.

GRIMOD DE LA REYNIERE, *Almanach des Gourmands*, 1803

Spinach is the broom of the stomach.

FRENCH PROVERB

Spinach: Acts on your stomach like a broom. Never forget to repeat M. Prudhomme's famous remark: "I don't like it, and am glad of it, because if I liked it I would eat it—and I can't stand it." (Some people will find this sensible enough and won't laugh.)

GUSTAVE FLAUBERT, 1821-1880, *Dictionnaire des Idées Reçu*

One man's poison ivy is another man's spinach.

GEORGE ADE, 1866-1944, *Hand-Made Fables*

Mother: It's broccoli, dear.
Child: I say it's spinach, and I say the hell with it.

CARL ROSE, Caption to a Cartoon in the *New Yorker*

If the man who turnip cries
Cries not when his father dies,
'Tis a proof that he had rather,
Have a turnip than his father.

SAMUEL JOHNSON, 1709-1784

The Apple of Love is called in Latine *Poma Ameris*, and *Lycopersicum*: of some *Glaucium*: in English, Apple of Love, and Golden Apples: in French, *Pommes d'amours.* Howbeit there be other golden Apples whereof the Poets doe fable, growing in the Gardens of the daughters of Hesperus, which a Dragon was appointed to keepe, who, as they fable, was killed by Hercules.

The Golden Apple, with the whole herbe it selfe is cold, yet not so fully so cold as Mandrake, after the opinion of Dodonaeus. But in my judgement it is very cold, yea perhaps in the highest degree of coldnesse: my reason is, because I have in the hottest time of Summer cut away the superfluous branches of the mother root, and cast them away carelessly in the allies of my Garden, the which (nothwithstanding the extreme heate of the Sun, the hardnesse of the trodden allies, and at that time when no rain at all did fal) have growne as fresh where I cast them, as before I did cut them off; which argueth the great coldnesse contained therein. True it is, that it doth argue also a great moisture wherewith this the plant is possessed, but as I have said, not without great cold, which I leave to every mans censure.

In Spaine and those hot Regions they use to eate the Apples prepared and boiled with pepper, and oyle: but they yeeld very little nourishment to the body, and the same naught and corrupt.

Likewise they doe eate the Apples with oile, vinegre and pepper mixed together for sauce to their meat, even as we in these cold countries doe Mustard.

JOHN GERARD, 1545-1607, *Herball*

of FRUIT & CHEESE

In an orchard there should be enough to eat, enough to lay up, enough to be stolen, and enough to rot upon the ground.

JAMES BOSWELL, ascribed to Dr. Madden in *Life of Johnson,* 1783

Tell me what fruit is bitter when ripe, delightful when green, and sweet when half-ripe? HINDI PROVERB

Ab ovo usque ad mala.
From the eggs to the apples. A Latin saying corresponding to our "from soup to nuts."

JUVENAL, 60?-?140, *Satires*

An apple a day keeps the doctor away.

ENGLISH PROVERB

Comfort me with apples: for I am sick of love.

Solomon's Song ii, 5, *c.* 200

He pares his apple that will cleanly feed.

GEORGE HERBERT, 1593-1633, *The Temple*

An apple, an egg and a nut
You may eat after a slut.

JOHN RAY, 1627-1705, *English Proverbs*

The apple grows so bright and high,
And ends its days in apple-pie.

SAMUEL HOFFENSTEIN, 1890-1947, *Songs About Life*

I loathe, abhor, despise,
Abominate dried apple pies . . .
But of all poor grub beneath the skies,
The poorest is dried apple pies . . .
Tread on my corns, or tell me lies,
But don't pass me dried apple pies.   ANONYMOUS

Coleridge holds that a man cannot have a pure mind
who refuses apple-dumplings. I am not certain but
what he is right.   CHARLES LAMB, 1775-1834, *Essays of Elia*

Solon, in an attempt to stop the extravagant expense
of weddings, ordained that newlyweds should eat

nothing but one apple each before going to the marriage bed; which was scarcely substantial comfort for the poor couples.   ALEXANDRE DUMAS, 1802-1870

All millionaires love a baked apple.
RONALD FIRBANK, 1886-1926, *Vainglory*

And for an apple damn'd mankind.
THOMAS OTWAY, 1652-1685, *The Orphan*

Animals of all kinds, including even cats, are fond of this fruit.
J. B. LAVAT, *Nouveau voyage aux îles de l'Amérique*, 1722

Where the banana grows man is sensual and cruel.
R. W. EMERSON, 1803-1882,
Society and Solitude

Yes, we have no bananas.
FRANK SILVER, Title of Song, 1923

. . . The young buds or tender tops of the bramble bush, the floures, the leaves, and the unripe fruit, being chewed, stay all manner of bleedings. They heale the eies that hang out.

The ripe fruit is sweet, and containeth in it much juyce of a temperate heate, therefore it is not unpleasant to be eaten.

The leaves of the Bramble boyled in water, with honey, allum, and a little white wine added thereto, make a most excellent lotion or washing water, and the same decoction fastneth the teeth.

JOHN GERARD, 1545-1612, *Herball*

I am going to turn over a new life and am going to be a very good girl and be obedient to Isa Keith, here there is plenty of gooseberries which makes my teeth watter.   MARJORIE FLEMING, 1803-1811, *Journal*

A grapefruit is a lemon that had a chance and took advantage of it.   AUTHOR UNIDENTIFIED

I am sure the grapes are sour.   AESOP, *c.* 550 B.C.

The fathers have eaten a sour grape, and the children's teeth are set on edge.   *Jeremiah* xxxi, 29

Orange:
Cheerfully adorn the proudest table,
Since yours it is to bear the glorious label—
"Richest in Vitamins!"   ROSE FYLEMAN, 1877-1957

The ripest peach is highest on the tree.

JAMES WHITCOMB RILEY, 1849-1916

Rightly thought of there is poetry in peaches . . .
even when they are canned.

H. GRANVILLE-BARKER, 1877-1946, *The Madras House*

Eating pears cleans the teeth.   KOREAN PROVERB

A pear must be eaten to the day;
If you don't eat it then, throw it away.
OLD ENGLISH RHYME

Strawberry: Doubtless God could have made a better berry, but doubtless God never did.
Quoted by IZAAK WALTON, 1593-1683, *The Compleat Angler*

May they have sugar to their strawberries.
LEIGH HUNT, 1784-1859

Toujours strawberries and cream.
SAMUEL JOHNSON, 1709-1784,
complaining to his hostess, Mrs. Thrale

Cheese—milk's leap toward immortality.
CLIFTON FADIMAN, 1904- , *Any Number Can Play*

Cheese it is a peevish elf,
It digests all things but itself.
Caseus est nequam
quia, digerit omnia sequam.
JOHN RAY, 1627-1705, *A Collection of English Proverbs*

Quote Brillat-Savarin's maxim: "Dessert without cheese is like a beauty with only one eye."
GUSTAVE FLAUBERT, 1821-1880, *Dictionnaire des Idées Reçu*

Cheese and salt meat should be sparingly eat.
BENJAMIN FRANKLIN, 1706-1790, *Poor Richard's Almanack*

An apple-pie without some cheese
Is like a kiss without a squeeze.

OLD ENGLISH RHYME

But I, when I undress me
  Each night, upon my knees
Will ask the Lord to bless me
  With apple pie and cheese.

EUGENE FIELD, 1850-1895, *Apple Pie and Cheese*

A tiny bit of Camembert!
What strange illusions linger there!
What visions direful and distressed
Through hours that should be sweet with rest!

PHILANDER JOHNSON, 1866-1939,
A Fromage Phantasy

Hi! James—let loose the Gorgonzola!   *Punch*, 1889

Botticelli isn't a wine, you Juggins! Botticelli's a
cheese.   *Punch*, 1894

Many's the long night I've dreamed of cheese—
toasted, mostly.

R. L. STEVENSON, 1850-1894, *Treasure Island*

The moon is made of green cheese.   ENGLISH PROVERB

A woman had such an antipathy against cheese that
if she but eat a piece of bread, cut with a knife which

a little before had cut cheese, it would cause a deliquium.
                    INCREASE MATHER, 1639-1723, *Remarkable Providences*

How can you be expected to govern a country that has two hundred and forty-six kinds of cheese?
          CHARLES DE GAULLE, 1890-1972, *Newsweek*, Oct. 1, 1962

After cheese comes nothing.   ENGLISH PROVERB

O{ FINGERBOWLS

Sign of wealth in the household.
          GUSTAVE FLAUBERT, 1821-1880, *Dictionnaire des Idées Reçu*

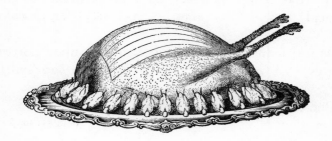

o𝑓 FEASTS & FEASTING

Enough is as good as a feast.
JOHN HEYWOOD, 1497?-1580?, *Proverbs*

Feasts must be solemn and rare, or else they cease to
be feasts.   ALDOUS HUXLEY, 1894-1963, *Do What You Will*

Small cheer and great welcome makes a merry feast.
WILLIAM SHAKESPEARE, 1564-1616, *The Comedy of Errors*

But, first
Or last, your fine Egyptian cookery
Shall have the fame. I have heard that
  Julius Caesar
Grew fat with feasting there.
WILLIAM SHAKESPEARE, 1564-1616, *Antony and Cleopatra*

He that banquets every day, never makes a good
meal.   THOMAS FULLER, 1608-1661, *Gnomologia*

Be not made a beggar by banqueting upon borrow-
ings.   *Ecclesiastes* xviii, 33

One cannot both feast and become rich.
                                   ASHANTI PROVERB

Fools makes feasts, and wise men eat them.
                  THOMAS FULLER, 1608-1661, *Gnomologia*

We have a trifling foolish banquet towards.
          WILLIAM SHAKESPEARE, 1564-1616, *Romeo and Juliet*

Spare Feast! a radish and an egg.
                WILLIAM COWPER, 1731-1800, *The Task*

Dutch feast: where the entertainer gets drunk before
his guests.   FRANCIS GROSE, 1731?-1791,
                   A Classical Dictionary of the Vulgar Tongue

There is no great banquet but some fares ill.
            GEORGE HERBERT, 1593-1633, *Outlandish Proverbs*

Lasciviousness, lusts, excess of wine, revellings,
banquetings.   *I Peter* iv, 3, *c.* 60

Some men are born to feast, and not to fight;
Whose sluggish minds, e'en in fair honor's field,

Still on their dinner turn—
Let such pot-boiling varlets stay at home,
And wield a flesh-hook rather than a sword.

JOANNA BAILLIE, 1762-1851, Basil

As much Valor is to be found in feasting as in fighting, and some of our city captains and carpet knights
will make this good, and prove it.

ROBERT BURTON, 1577-1640, Anatomy of Melancholy

Our first and second course being three score dishes
at one board, and after that always a banquet.

JOHN TAYLOR, 1580-1653, Pennyles Pilgrimage

The heads of parrots, tongues of nightingales,
The brains of peacocks, and of ostriches,
Shall be our food; and could we get the phoenix,
Though nature lost her kind, she were our dish.

BEN JONSON, 1573?-1637, Volpone

My footboy shall eat pheasants, calver'd salmons,
Knots, godwits, lampreys; I myself will have
The beards of barbels serv'd instead of salads,
Oil'd mushrooms, and the swelling unctuous paps
Of a fat pregnant sow, newly cut off.

BEN JONSON, 1573?-1637, The Alchemist

I have been a great observer and I can truly say that
I have known a man "fond of good eating and drinking," as it is called; that I have never known such a

man (and hundreds I have known) who was not
worthy of respect.

WILLIAM COBBETT, 1763-1835, *Advice to Young Men*

Nice eaters seldom meet with a good dinner.

THOMAS FULLER, 1608-1661, *Gnomologia*

They were at once dainty and voracious, understood
the right and wrong of every dish, and alike emptied
the one and the other.

FRANCES BURNEY, 1752-1840, *Evelina*

Gourmets dig their graves with their teeth.

FRENCH PROVERB

I have never been anything so refined as a *gourmet*;
so I am happy to say that I am still quite capable of
being a glutton. My ignorance of cookery is such
that I can even eat the food in the most fashionable
and expensive hotels in London.

G. K. CHESTERTON, 1874-1936, *Autobiography*

It is not greedy to enjoy a good dinner, any more
than it is greedy to enjoy a good concert. But I do
think there is something greedy about trying to
enjoy the concert and dinner at the same time.

G. K. CHESTERTON, 1874-1936, *Generally Speaking*

I am gluttony. My parents are all dead, and the devil
a penny they have left me, but a bare pension, and

that is thirty meals a day—a small trifle to suffice nature. I come of a royal parentage! My grandfather was a gammon of bacon, my grandmother a hogshead of claret wine.

CHRISTOPHER MARLOWE, 1564-1593, *Dr Faustus*

Towards freshness or presumption he was unmerciful. . . . There was a lady once who ventured an impertinence. Sitting next Trollope at dinner she noticed that he partook largely of every dish offered to him. "You seem to have a very good appetite, Mr. Trollope," she observed. "None at all, Madam," he replied, "but thank God, I am very greedy."

MICHAEL SADLEIR, 1888-1957, *Trollope: A Commentary*

I am not hungry; but thank goodness, I am greedy.

Punch, 1878

Gluttony is less common among women than among men. Women commonly eat more sparingly and are less curious in the choice of meat; but if once you find a woman gluttonous, expect from her very little virtue.

SAMUEL JOHNSON, 1709-1784, In Mrs. Piozzi's *Autobiography*

Gluttony hinders chastity.

POPE XYSTUS I, *The Ring, c.* 150

Great eaters and great sleepers are incapable of anything else that is great.   HENRY IV OF FRANCE, 1553-1610

For two nights the glutton cannot sleep for thinking, first on an empty stomach, and next on a sated stomach. SA'DI, *Gulistan*, 1258

Two hungry meals make the third a glutton. JOHN HEYWOOD, 1497?-1580, *Proverbs*

Gluttony slays more than the sword. ENGLISH PROVERB

Who hastens a glutton chokes him. GEORGE HERBERT, 1593-1633, *Outlandish Proverbs*

It is easier to fill a glutton's belly than his eye. THOMAS FULLER, 1608-1661, *Gnomologia*

He hath eaten me out of house and home. WILLIAM SHAKESPEARE, 1564-1616, *Henry IV*

None is happy but a glutton. JOHN LYLY, 1554?-1606, *A Serving Men's Song*

Enjoy yourselves, gluttons and guzzlers, fill up your bellies.
Vivite larcones, comedones, vivite ventris. G. LUCILIUS, *c.* 180-102 B.C.

of DIET

Pope hastened his death by feeding much on high-
seasoned dishes, and drinking spirits.

JOSEPH SPENCE, *Anecdotes*, 1858

To lengthen thy life, lessen thy meals.

BENJAMIN FRANKLIN, 1706-1790, *Poor Richard's Almanack*

Diet by measure, and defy the physician.

JOHN HEYWOOD, 1497?-1580?, *Proverbs*

The kitchen is a good apothecarie's shop.

WILLIAM BULLEIN, *The Bulwark against all Sickness*, 1562

Who eats of one dish never needs a physician.

ITALIAN PROVERB

Their best and most wholesome feeding is upon one dish and no more and the same plaine and simple: for surely this hudling of many meats one upon another of diverse tastes is pestiferous. But sundrie are more dangerous than that.

PLINY, 23-79, *Natural History*

Nature delights in the most plain and simple diet. Every animal but man keeps to one dish.

JOSEPH ADDISON, 1672-1719, *The Spectator*

Constantly practise abstinence and temperance so that you may be as wakeful after eating as before.

E. L. GRUBER, *Rules for the Examination of our Daily Lives*, 1715

Total abstinence is easier than perfect moderation.

ST. AUGUSTINE, 354-430, *On the Good of Marriage*

Fasting is better than prayer.

ST. CLEMENT, fl. late 1st century A.D.,
Second Epistle to the Corinthians

Fasting is a medicine.

ST. JOHN CHRYSOSTOM, 347-407, *Homilies*

Fasting today makes the food good tomorrow.

GERMAN PROVERB

I have noticed walking about the country that the children seem to eat much less than they require: it is hard to imagine so immoderate a passion for abstinence.   VOLTAIRE, 1694-1778, letter to M. de Bestide

A fast is better than a bad meal.   IRISH PROVERB

When I am here I do not fast on Saturday; when at Rome I do fast on Saturday.
                         ST. AUGUSTINE, 354-430, *Epistle* xxvi

He that feeds barely fasts sufficiently.
                         RANDLE COTGRAVE, died *c.* 1634,
                         French-English Dictionary

If you wish to grow thinner, diminish your dinner,
     And take light claret instead of pale ale;
Look down with utter contempt upon butter,
     And never touch bread till it's toasted—or stale.
                         H. S. LEIGH, *Carols of Cockaigne,* 1869

A little with quiet is the only diet.
                         GEORGE HERBERT, 1593-1633, *Outlandish Proverbs*

If you have formed the habit of checking on every new diet that comes along, you will find that, mercifully, they all blur together, leaving you with only one definite piece of information: french-fried potatoes are out.
                         JEAN KERR, 1923-   , *Please Don't Eat the Daisies*

What some call health, if purchased by perpetual anxiety about diet, isn't much better than tedious disease.   GEORGE DENNISON PRENTICE,
1802-1870, *Prenticeanna*

My soul is dark with stormy riot,
Directly traceable to diet.
     SAMUEL HOFFENSTEIN, 1890-1947,
Out of the Everywhere into the Here

There is enough acid in your stomach to burn a hole in the carpet.   Advertisement headline
for a digestive tablet, 20th Century

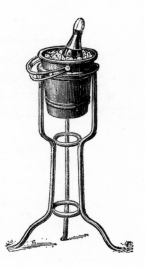

# of NIGHTCAPS

THOUGH its dispensers boast that the beverage called absinthe will strengthen the stomach and aid digestion, and though the Salerno school recommends absinthe for seasickness, it is impossible not to deplore its ravages among our poets and soldiers over the past forty years. There is not a regimental surgeon who will not tell you that absinthe has killed more Frenchmen in Africa than the *flitta*, the yataghan, and the guns of the Arabs put together.

Among our Bohemian poets absinthe has been called "the green muse." Several, and unfortunately not the poorest, have died from its poisoned embraces. Hégésippe Moreau, Amédée Roland, Alfred de Musset, our greatest poet after Hugo and Lamartine—all succcumbed to its disastrous effects.

De Musset's fatal passion for absinthe, which may have given some of his verses their bitter flavour, caused the dignified Academy to descend to punning. It seems that de Musset frequently found himself in no condition to attend the academic sessions. Which prompted one of the forty immortals to say that "he absinthes himself a bit too much."

ALEXANDRE DUMAS, 1802-1870,
Le Grand Dictionnaire de Cuisine

Ladies and Gentlemen I give you a toast. It is "absinthe makes the tart grow fonder."

Ascribed to HUGH DRUMMOND in
the *Vintage Years* by Seymour Hicks

Absinthe: Extra-violent passion: one glass and you're dead. Newspaper men drink it as they write their copy. Has killed more soldiers than the Bedouin.

GUSTAVE FLAUBERT, 1821-1880, *Dictionnaire des Idées Reçu*

People may say what they like about the decay of Christianity; the religious system that produced green Chartreuse can never really die.

SAKI, 1870-1916

Gin-and-water is the source of all my inspiration.

LORD BYRON, 1788-1824

You will find me drinking gin
In the lowest kind of inn,
Because I am a rigid Vegetarian.
        G. K. CHESTERTON, 1874-1936, *The Logical Vegetarian*

No gin, no king!
            Cry of the mob in London on the passage of an act
                    laying an excise tax on gin, 1736

Gin was mother's milk to her.
        G. B. SHAW, 1856-1950, *Pygmalion*

No man is genuinely happy, married, who has to
drink worse gin than he used to drink when he was
single.   H. L. MENCKEN, 1880-1956,
                                Prejudices, Fourth Series

There's naught, no doubt, so much the spirit calms,
As rum and true religion.
            LORD BYRON, 1788-1824, *Don Juan*

What butter or whiskey'll not cure, there's no cure
for.   IRISH PROVERB

Whiskey is good for snake-bite.
                        H. L. MENCKEN, 1880-1956 &
        GEORGE JEAN NATHAN, 1882-1958, *American Credo*

He'd go to mass every mornin' if holy water were
whiskey.   IRISH PROVERB

I like it: I always did, and that is the reason I never use it.   ROBERT E. LEE, 1807-1870,
on being ordered whiskey by his physician

Freedom and whiskey gang thegither.
ROBERT BURNS, 1759-1796, *The Author's Earnest Cry and Prayer*

I'd rather that England should be free than that England should be compulsorily sober.
ARCHBISHOP W. C. MAGEE, 1821-1891, Sermon at Peterborough

Where the corn is full of kernels
And colonels full of corn.
     W. J. LAMPTON, 1859-1917, *Kentucky*

Bernard always had a few prayers in the hall and some whiskey afterwards as he was rarther pious.
     DAISY ASHFORD, 1881-1972, *The Young Visitors*, 1919

Glass of brandy and water! That is the current but not the appropriate name: ask for a glass of liquid fire and distilled damnation.   ROBERT HALL, 1764-1831

There's some are fou o' love divine,
There' some are fou o' brandy.
     ROBERT BURNS, 1759-1796, *The Holy Fair*

A dose of brandy by stimulating the circulation, produces Dutch courage.
     HERBERT SPENCER, 1820-1903, *The Study of Sociology*

Claret is the liquor for boys; port for men; but he
who aspires to be a hero . . . must drink brandy.

SAMUEL JOHNSON, 1709-1784, Boswell's *Life*

Man can die
Much bolder with brandy.

JOHN GAY, 1685-1732, *The Beggar's Opera*

o THE COMPILER

Versed in the old court luxury, he knew,
The feasts of Nero, and his midnight crew;
Where, oft, when potent draughts had fired the brain,
The jaded taste, was spurr'd to gorge again.—
And, in my time, none understood so well,
The science of good eating: he could tell,
At the first relish, if his oysters fed
On the Rutupian, or the Lucrine bed;
And from a crab, or lobster's colour, name,
The country, nay the district, whence it came.

JUVENAL, 50-130 A.D., *Satire* iv

COLOPHON 175

This book is reproduced from the limited edition of 425 copies printed and published in 1975 by the Arion Press, San Francisco, under the direction of Andrew Hoyem, with the assistance of Linnea Gentry, Judith Hoyem, George F. Ritchie, and Glenn R. Todd. The types are Garamont, Narciss, and Typo Upright; the borders are Fournier; the vignettes are from wood engravings in *Ecole des Cuisinières*, Paris, *c.* 1870. This edition was printed by Maple-Vail on acid-free paper.